Creating a Safe & Friendly School

Lunchroom, Hallways,
Playground, and more ...

ARTICLES BY ELEMENTARY EDUCATORS

The stories in this book are all based on real events in the classroom. However, in order to respect the privacy of students, names and many identifying characteristics of students and situations have been changed.

ISBN-13: 978-1-892989-16-1
ISBN-10: 1-892989-16-6

Library of Congress control number: 2005935240

Project manager: Elizabeth Nash
Photographs: Peter Wrenn, David Detmold
Cover and book design: Helen Merena

Illustrations by elementary age children in Massachusetts

Northeast Foundation for Children, Inc.
85 Avenue A, Suite 204
P. O. Box 718
Turners Falls, MA 01376-0718

800-360-6332
www.responsiveclassroom.org

10 09 08 07 06   6 5 4 3 2 1

CONTENTS

CONTENTS

It's an early autumn morning at school, with 300 children gathered for an all-school meeting. The room buzzes with noise and movement as children find a spot to sit, the younger ones squirming and giggling and the older ones high-fiving their friends. Everyone scoots this way and that as more students squeeze in. Then the principal moves to the front of the room and silently raises her hand to signal for quiet and attention. This is the same signal that students use in their classrooms, on the playground, and in the lunchroom. The first students who see the raised hand copy it to help spread the signal, becoming quiet as they do so. Within seconds, bodies are stilled and turned toward the speaker; voices are hushed. Everyone's attention is on the principal. "Good morning, Crescent Valley School," she says warmly. "Good morning, Mrs. B.," the audience choruses back. Efficiently and calmly the stage has been set for a productive meeting.

It's hard to overstate the importance of a positive school-wide climate on children's school life. True, the individual classroom is the primary influence on a child's learning: Children learn best when their classrooms are places where they feel safe, known, and valued, places that free them to learn.

But classrooms are not entities unto themselves. Rather, they exist as part of a larger school, and the climate of that larger school can either support all that teachers are working to achieve in their classrooms, or undermine it. If in the classroom we teach the quiet signal as an important step in showing respect to others, then in all-school settings we need to use a similar signal to reinforce the message. If in the classroom we tell students that mistakes are opportunities to learn to do better next time, then on the playground we need to respond to children's mistakes with respectful, reasonable logical

INTRODUCTION

consequences that require them to help fix, rather than pay for, problems they caused. We notice and address sarcasm in literature circle; we must also notice and address a put-down on the playing field or a shove in the lunch line. Without this consistency, we risk leaving children confused as to what rules are at play. Worse, we risk teaching children that their classroom is an anomaly and that they'd better deal with the outer world in a different way, perhaps by dominating or by hiding.

From using a school-wide signal for quiet to establishing school-wide rules—and consequences for breaking them—we can do the most to nurture children's learning by ensuring that the same expectations and approaches govern behavior inside and outside the classroom.

This book offers seventeen articles about achieving this kind of school-wide consistency. They are excerpted from the *Responsive Classroom®* newsletter and other Northeast Foundation for Children (NEFC) publications. The articles provide snapshots of various schools' efforts to create a climate of trust, respect, and caring in hallways, playgrounds, bathrooms, lunchrooms, special area classrooms, all-school meeting areas, and other spaces beyond the classroom.

This book is not a comprehensive treatment of the subject of school-wide climate. Instead, it's a collection of ideas that teachers and administrators can think about for their own schools. You may find that many practices perfectly suited for another school also work just as beautifully in your own. Or you may find that you need to do a bit of adapting to suit the particular character, needs, and resources of your school. We offer these ideas for you to consider as you continue on your path to providing the best possible learning environment for your students.

—*Alice Yang,* NEFC PUBLICATIONS MANAGER

Creating a
Safe & Friendly
School

The Bus

The Wheels on the Bus

*A principal involves students in improving behavior
and ensuring safety on the bus ride to school*

BY PAMELA ROBERTS

FREELANCE EDUCATIONAL RESEARCHER AND WRITER

School bus safety affects some 23 million students nation-wide who collectively travel 4 billion miles a year. From the parent in Buffalo, New York, who drives her children to school because they are afraid of being bullied by the older kids, to the teacher in Island Falls, Maine, who takes her kindergartners out to sit on the bus and talk about safety, there are nationwide concerns about the physical and emotional well-being of students on the bus. And while national debate centers on seat belt usage, the emotional safety of children is rarely addressed.

Growing concerns about the well-being of children on the school bus inspired Marcia Bradley, principal of Wellfleet Elementary School, a K-5 school in Wellfleet, Massachusetts, to take a proactive approach to school bus safety.

"Basically you're just tossing a bunch of kids into a big yellow tin can," Bradley says about her motivation for addressing this issue more intensively. "It's very unstructured. It's like lunchroom and recess: it's one of the places where unkind things can happen." Bradley could see that youngsters were upset when they came into school, and their feelings affected what happened in the classroom.

AN IDEA EMERGES

During a week-long *Responsive Classroom*® institute in 1997, Bradley and another principal in attendance, Greg Bagley of Southern Aroostook Community School in Island Falls, Maine, both confronting similar problems, came up with an idea for involving the children in improving behavior and ensuring safety on their bus ride.

Rather than simply telling children what to do, teachers would guide students in making observations about the bus and build on this knowledge through hands-on activities and discussion. Later, when rules about bus behavior were generated and discussed, children would have a clear understanding of the purposes behind the rules. "It's a way to raise children's awareness about bus safety and to give them an opportunity to think about, and talk about, their choices on the bus," says Bradley.

In her six years at Wellfleet, Bradley had tried to improve the children's bus behavior in a variety of ways—reviewing bus rules, talking to students, having them draw pictures—but had no long-term success until she started using this approach three years ago.

Now she sees a huge improvement in students' bus behavior. The number of reports for bus misconduct has plummeted from an average of two a week to only one every three or four weeks.

A Safer, Smoother Ride

More ideas for what teachers can do

1 "Talk about all of the places in the school, including the bus, as being part of the school community," says Marcia Bradley, principal of Wellfleet Elementary School, who conducts a school bus guided observation with students each year. "Let the children know that the same expectations apply on the bus as everywhere else. This is ongoing throughout the year."

2 Assign bus buddies so that children know whom they'll sit with. If possible, pair younger and older students so that the older children help to take care of the younger ones. This helps break the pattern of older children wanting certain seats or other special treatment.

3 When conflicts arise, talk with the class about the problems, brainstorm ways to solve them, and roleplay the solutions when appropriate.

4 Have the school bus drivers come to Morning Meeting or to an all-school meeting so that children get to know them. Raise the children's awareness that the bus driver's job is to drive them safely to and from school, not to monitor their behavior.

5 Help children find activities that will occupy them positively on the bus, such as drawing, doing homework, or reading. Play some travel games in Morning Meeting that students could play on the bus. Provide materials such as clipboards, markers, and paper.

6 If a child does get a bus report for improper conduct, discuss it with him or her and make a plan for improvement.

"Children come off the bus happy now. They have a nice time being with their friends."

Here's how the approach works.

OBSERVATION: "IT HAS BIG TIRES!"

Before taking each class to observe and ride the bus, Bradley visits the classrooms. She talks with students about her goals for the bus ride and asks them how they would like the bus ride to be. She then leads the students, clipboards in hand, outside for a guided observation of the bus.

This morning, Bradley leads a group of second and third graders. The children stand in two lines in front of the bus. "This is an opportunity to notice as many things about the bus as you can," Bradley says to the children. "And it is an opportunity to share our ideas with one another. So before we start, can you tell me, just standing here, what you notice?"

"It's very yellow!" says a voice.

"It has BIG tires!"

"There are a lot of lights … twenty-one lights on the back!"

"I see an emergency exit door."

Bradley points out the safety zone around the bus and explains why it's there: "So you are not too close to the road and not too close to the bus, because we don't want anyone to get hurt." She then gives the children permission—just during this observation—to walk closer to the bus than the safety zone allows.

The third grade students divide into small groups and take clipboards and paper. They write down their observations as they explore the outside of the bus. The second graders report their observations to their teacher, who writes them down. One child peers under the bus and notices the motor. Another finds the height of the wheel to be just right for him to use as a desk as he writes down what his classmates say.

"I notice this," says a second grader, pointing to a yellow bar on the front of the bus. Driver Regis Butilier shows the children how the yellow safety bar swings out. "This was added on a couple of years ago to make sure everyone stays in the safety zone in front of the bus," she says. "Always walk so the driver can see you, and walk straight across."

After ten minutes the students line up again in preparation for boarding the bus. "When we go on our ride, our job is to notice what our driver does," Bradley says. "And, remember, when we get on the bus, you're going to show me how to sit safely."

After a short ride, the third graders return to their classroom to share what they have noticed. Their teacher, Jan LaTanzi, writes down their observations on a chart in the front of the room. "I noticed an emergency exit," says one student. "I noticed when the driver stopped at the stop sign I could hear the brakes," says another.

Fire extinguisher, first aid kit, stop sign on the side of the bus, license plate—LaTanzi leads the children in a brief discussion of each item as it comes up.

"How come the bus had a seat belt for the driver and not for passengers?" one child asks, hitting upon the national controversy about seat belts in school buses.

"This has been discussed all across the country, whether or not we should have seat belts," LaTanzi says. "Massachusetts has not made a ruling yet."

From the Bus to the Classroom

The "Morning Program" at Cortland, New York

EXCERPTED FROM

TIME TO TEACH, TIME TO LEARN: CHANGING THE PACE OF SCHOOL, BY CHIP WOOD

PUBLISHED BY NORTHEAST FOUNDATION FOR CHILDREN, 1999

In the Cortland, New York, elementary schools, what began as a response to problems when buses arrived and students had to wait on the playground has become a strong part of the learning community's culture. Now, when students come off the bus, they go directly to the cafeteria for breakfast or into the gym for "Morning Program." Morning Program begins with supervised physical activity and music as the gym fills up with more and more bus arrivers and breakfast finishers.

Principals are in the gym, "directing traffic" and greeting students. A Morning Program Committee of upper grade students readies a formal and set agenda. At a word from the principal over the sound system (the principal wears a lavaliere microphone), all students sit by classes or grade level groups. The Morning Program Committee and the principal swing into action. Birthdays are celebrated, academic projects are shared by a class, special announcements are made, and occasional special guests lead an activity. Finally, everyone stands and salutes the flag, sings a song, and heads off to their own classroom and their own individual Morning Meetings.

I have never seen a better example of character education at the school district level. It is a daily example of a school culture where respect, responsibility, and civility are central to an exciting learning process.

CREATING BUS RULES WITH THE CHILDREN

At an all-school meeting held after the observation, the children collectively come up with their own rules for the bus ride. First they collect all the observation sheets and charts and put them in a book just the way they are written.

"This activity makes them part of the process," says LaTanzi. "Their ideas are valued. Having the clipboard and writing down their observations gives them a sense of importance about their observations, and they remember more."

Next they talk about the implications of all the things they have noticed about the bus. The bus has huge front windows? That's so the driver can see well. They share what they've observed about the bus driver and talk about the importance of him/her being able to drive without distractions. Children's awareness of the bus driver is raised and they learn that although the driver's job is to get them safely to and from school, their job is to help the driver by monitoring their own behavior.

Safe school bus behavior—what it sounds like, looks like, feels like—is explicitly discussed. What can you do to help the driver do his/her job? What kinds of voices should you use on the bus? How should you sit? What should you do if you need help? Finally, students, with guidance from adults, come up with three or four rules, which are posted and referred to throughout the year.

CHILDREN BUILD AUTONOMY

As a result of these steps—introducing how to behave on the school bus, exploring the bus, discussing what was noticed, and then generating rules—the students "recognize the reasons for the rules," Bradley says. "Now the children can get on the bus without somebody directing every move they make. They are more aware of their behavior and more motivated to stay in control." Pam Porter, director of consulting services at Northeast Foundation for Children, echoes Bradley's thought. "This approach helps children build autonomy," she says. "It puts kids in charge and builds on their knowledge." Porter feels the success is also due to the fact that the children observed and thought about the driver and "that's the beginning of a relationship." She adds, "It helps them to build empathy and to think about the impact of their behavior."

The bus drivers at Wellfleet Elementary agree. As one says, "We like this approach; it's a big help to us. It makes us feel that the school respects us and our job."

WHAT'S NEXT? A BUDDY SYSTEM

The behavior on the school buses at Wellfleet is still not entirely satisfactory to Bradley, however. There are still some complaints that the bus is too noisy and that older students bother younger ones. Bradley hopes to address these concerns by pairing up older students with younger ones as bus buddies. She has noticed some of the older children starting to be more supportive of the younger ones and wants to build on this in the future.

Porter sees this as an important direction to explore. "One of the things that's true about the bus ride is that the older children are in a position to do essential community work by looking after the younger kids on the bus," she says. "So often what children are told is that you have to take care of yourselves. What they need to hear is that everyone has to take care of each other."

FROM THE SUMMER 2000 ISSUE OF THE *RESPONSIVE CLASSROOM* NEWSLETTER.

Working toward Bus Civility

BY CHIP WOOD

NEFC CO–FOUNDER AND PRINCIPAL AT SHEFFIELD ELEMENTARY SCHOOL

TURNERS FALLS, MASSACHUSETTS

B ehavior on the bus has always challenged children's developing abilities of self-control, not to mention the patience of bus drivers, parents, and principals. The truth of the matter is that nowhere is children's misbehavior and mistreatment of each other more ignored than on the school bus.

For the most part, bus monitors, closed-circuit TV monitors, bus detentions, and suspensions have not resulted in long-term learning or significant changes in student conduct. Furthermore, these methods are expensive, time consuming, and often inconsistent; the follow-up is spotty; and children often become quite savvy about what they can "get away with" on the bus.

How can we as administrators, teachers, parents, and all other adults on "bus duty" show children that we care about what happens on the bus? How can we help them behave calmly and respectfully on the ride to and from school?

Here are two possible strategies.

REFLECTION AND REHEARSAL AT THE END OF THE DAY

First, we can take time at the end of the school day to prepare students for the bus ride coming up. The end of the day is seldom used proactively to help children make the transition to their next activity or environment. I know that when I was a teacher, I was often guilty of teaching right up to the last minute, getting in one more idea or spending just a little more time going over the homework assignment, even after the bus calls had started. I didn't pay attention to what the children needed most at that moment.

I now recommend that teachers try to end the school day ten minutes before the buses are called, to have the cleanup done, the homework explained, and any notices going home already in the backpacks. Teachers can then gather the children in a quiet circle to reflect about the day and rehearse the bus ride coming up.

This simple check-in can make a big difference. For example:

✦ A teacher says, "Bus calls will start in five minutes, Jeremy. What do you plan to do on your bus ride home today?" This may be just the right amount of rehearsal to enable Jeremy to make the bus trip without getting into conflicts.

✦ A teacher announces, "Students on Bus Three, I'd like to see you on the meeting rug for five minutes. The rest of you can read your library books quietly." This could give the teacher time to model and role-play with children on this bus what they need to remember during their ride to their after-school program.

I acknowledge that this is the hardest time of day for the teacher to be proactive. The teacher is tired. The children are tired. The person on the loudspeaker is tired. But the reward for mustering this last little bit of energy will be that the children will be able to behave more calmly and responsibly on the bus ride home.

MORNING BUS PROGRAM BEFORE THE SCHOOL DAY STARTS

The second strategy has to do with the opposite end of the day. The moments after buses unload in the morning are a great time to do some proactive teaching about bus behavior. Whatever happened that day on the bus—good or bad—is fresh on children's minds. So why not conduct a daily morning bus program during that time for children to reflect, debrief, or do some real problem solving around bus issues?

This was the strategy that I introduced at a small K–8 school in Massachusetts years ago when I was the principal there. Because the town was rural, many children had to ride the bus for up to forty-five minutes, more than enough time for bus problems to erupt.

I used chairs to set up a "practice bus" in the cafeteria. Each day, I took one busload of children there while children from the other buses went on to their classrooms to start their day as usual.

The children who came with me would talk about that morning's bus ride. If it was a nice ride, we'd talk about what made it nice. "How did kids talk? What were some friendly words they said? What kind of voice did they use? How did they sit in the seats?" With chairs set up to simulate a bus, children could easily demonstrate the positive behaviors. This conscious reflection and debriefing powerfully reinforces for children not just the importance of being friendly and respectful, but how to be friendly and respectful.

If the morning's ride was not so nice, we'd talk about what made it not nice. Here I'd have to carefully guide the children to keep the conversation constructive and not let it deteriorate into finger pointing or tattling. If necessary, we would do some conflict resolution, perhaps involving role playing. (Of course, if there had been a fight or specific conflict involving just a few students, I'd separately address that problem with those students.) Conversations like these give children ideas for how to make bus rides go better in the future. Just as importantly, the children have time to cool down before starting their school day.

A common dilemma for schools wanting to try this strategy, of course, is that mornings are the busiest time of day for administrators. When you have announcements to make and parents to see, and no one is available to cover breakfast, it's hard to stop and deal with a busload of children.

One solution is to share the task of conducting the morning bus program with other school staff: the physical education teacher, the Title I teacher, the health teacher, a recess or lunch teacher—any staff other than regular classroom teachers. Whatever the setup, the job of the morning bus program leader is to create the space, spirit, and energy for practicing bus civility.

A GOOD INVESTMENT OF TIME

This kind of intervention takes time and planning. But dealing with bus problems reactively is also time-consuming. If we don't invest in preventing bus problems, we will likely continue to spend our time instead on suspensions, family conferences, and bus company meetings. The children's bus experience will also continue to be largely negative.

This is true for all the other areas of school life as well, be they recess, lunch, the hallways, or the bathroom. When we help children practice what we expect, we can expect more.

The Bus Bully Project

*Third and fifth graders take action
on a school-wide problem*

BY PAMELA ROBERTS

FREELANCE EDUCATIONAL RESEARCHER AND WRITER

O ver the years, third grade teacher Karen Lefave had become increasingly concerned about how the morning bus ride affected her students at Brayton Elementary School in North Adams, Massachusetts. "Bullying on the bus set the tone for the whole day and often left my third graders in tears," she said. She also saw her students dawdling at the end of the day, trying to avoid riding the bus back home. When Lefave took a course on using community service learning (CSL) in the classroom, she realized that CSL could help her address the bus bully problem. CSL combines students' service to the community with academic learning. In Lefave's case, the community served would be the school.

Lefave approached school adjustment counselor Nancy Gallagher, who also was frustrated with trying to address the school bus problems. They realized that eradicating bus misbehavior was beyond the scope of one CSL project. But they also knew they didn't need to fix everything at once. They could begin with one CSL project as an important first step in addressing the problems.

A PROJECT IS BORN

Lefave and Gallagher began talking about general bus concerns with the students in Lefave's classroom. The children discussed their bus worries and drew pictures and wrote stories about them. For a week, the students recorded examples of bullying behavior such as name-calling, pushing, teasing, and yelling. Then they brainstormed: What can be done to make things better?

INVOLVING FIFTH GRADERS

As the third graders investigated the problem, it became apparent that older students were the ones who were doing much of the bullying. What if, the third graders wondered, we got some of the big children on our side? Lefave and Gallagher identified five fifth graders who would be beneficial to the project. Twice a week, during language arts period, the third and fifth graders discussed what bullying felt like and why some people might bully other people.

Breaking up into groups of six or seven, each group having a fifth grader in it, children role-played bullying behavior, its outcomes, and possible ways to prevent it. Some children learned that they had the power to say "stop" to bullying behavior; others learned they could walk away or get help from an adult.

As a result, bullying behavior on the bus decreased and children felt safer. In fact, student responses to a pre- and post-project sur-

vey showed a significant drop in the number of third graders who said that they worried about being on the bus.

INVOLVING BUS DRIVERS

An unexpected outcome of all the talk about the bullying happening on the buses was that the bus drivers felt blamed and unsupported and wanted their side to be heard. Seeing the importance of addressing the drivers' concerns, Lefave and Gallagher planned a follow-up CSL project in which bus drivers would have a role.

Meanwhile, one thing the two educators had learned from the first project was that the problems on the bus weren't necessarily created by the expected "troublemakers." "It was everybody," said Gallagher.

So in the second year's project, which involved a new class of third graders and a whole class of fifth graders, the teachers brainstormed with the children about why so many children "go bananas" on the bus. Students reasoned that it had to do with anonymity—they didn't have a relationship with the bus driver. "Kids realized that they don't act this way in class because they know their teacher. What if they were to know their bus driver?" said Lefave.

The children decided to interview the drivers. They came up with a list of questions, practiced interviewing, and then made appointments with the eight bus drivers for interviews and picture taking. With the information from their interviews and the photos, the children made posters and hung them all over the school. "Meet the driver of the Flower Bus," said a typical poster. "His name is Mr. Wilson. He has a dog. He likes to travel."

CREATING CHILD-FRIENDLY BUS RULES

Also during this second year, students focused on another important reason why children behave better in the classroom than on the bus—because the classroom has rules. Did the bus have rules?

Yes. But because of the way the rules were written, the students couldn't understand them. Sentences such as "Do not behave in a boisterous manner" and "If seats are not available, proceed toward the rear of the bus, remain standing in the middle aisle, and grasp a seat bar firmly," while crucial, didn't mean much to the children. So the students took on the project of rewriting the bus rules in child-friendly language. With some funding from a $300 mini-grant from the school district, and with the help of a parent who did the graphics, the class made copies of the kid-friendly rules and distributed them to all the students in the school.

A DAY TO CELEBRATE

The culmination of this second year's project was "Bus Driver Appreciation Day," to which the children invited the drivers, the whole school, and the press. The children also asked the rest of the school to make appreciation posters.

At the end of the celebration, the whole school met outside on the grass. The children who had interviewed the drivers greeted them,

introduced them to the school community, said one thing they
had learned about the drivers, and presented them with flowers.
Then everyone gave the drivers three cheers of "Hip, hip, hooray."
"The bus drivers were beaming," said Lefave.

LOOKING BACK AT THE TWO YEARS

The two years' worth of work had positive results: Behavior inci-
dents reported by bus drivers were cut in half. Equally important,
the students grew academically and socially.

Noting that the projects empowered both her students and her-
self, Lefave said that her students became young social activists
ready to tackle a long list of projects. "They wanted to take on
the world after this," she said.

In addition to learning they could make a difference, students
used a range of academic skills. In the course of the project, they
wrote in their journals, shared entries, wrote letters, composed
short skits for role-playing activities, created a brochure of bus
rules, and spoke in front of an audience—all of which called on
language arts skills. In identifying and recording bullying behavior,
they learned the process of scientific inquiry and observation.
Throughout the project, they practiced the important social skills
of active listening, empathy, and assertion.

Finally, many children benefited from the pairing of younger and
older students. Working with fifth graders gave the third graders
something to aspire to. Conversely, the pairing allowed the fifth
graders to take care of the third graders by being role models. As
one fifth grader wrote: "I am learning that ... I should set a better
example on the bus, since I am a fifth grader and students look up
to me."

FROM THE SPRING 2002 ISSUE OF THE *RESPONSIVE CLASSROOM* NEWSLETTER.

Hallways and Bathrooms

Calm, Friendly Hallway Behavior

BY SADIE FISCHESSER

NEFC STAFF MEMBER

A whistle blows, signaling that the day is about to begin at Four Corners Elementary School in Greenfield, Massachusetts. The children scamper to organize themselves into grade-level lines. On an adult's signal, one line moves toward the building, pausing at the door. "We are about to go inside. What kind of waves will we use?" the adult asks the students. "Quiet, friendly waves," one child volunteers. "Why those kinds of waves?" A kindergartner replies, "Because there's no room for big waves or big voices."

With that, the adult asks, "Are we ready?" The children nod, and the line moves into the building and down the hallway. The adult walks at the back of the line.

As lines of students enter the hallway and go toward their classrooms, they pass teachers standing outside the classroom doors. Each teacher greets the students with a smile and a wave or a high five. The calm, quiet, and upbeat atmosphere sets a positive tone for the day.

This calm, friendly scene is typical of hallway transitions at Four Corners Elementary. Whether it's going to specials, coming in from recess, heading to lunch, or leaving at dismissal, the students know what's expected of them and, with few exceptions, live up to the expectations.

But this wasn't always the case. Hallways at Four Corners used to be loud and rough. Students would push each other; fights would break out. Ten years ago, the faculty decided to make a change. They wanted the school, including its hallways, to be a welcoming and safe place for children to learn.

SETTING EXPECTATIONS

The teachers and staff agreed to start small—and start with themselves. They agreed that each morning every adult would come into the hallway, greet one another, and greet the students coming into the building.

From there, they established expectations for hallway behavior for adults and students. Today, the expectations of adults are:

✦ Greet all students and adults around the school.

✦ Model positive, responsible behavior with colleagues and students.

✦ Ensure that all students have a pass when out of the classroom.

✦ Ask any visitor without a visitor pass to check in at the office.

And the expectations of students are:

✦ Use walking feet in the hallway.

✦ Stop at intervals to check with the adult for instructions
to continue or wait.

✦ Keep hands and feet to yourself.

✦ Use quiet voices to respect other classes that are working.

These rules are now part of the school culture. Kate Marion
LaPierre, the school behavior specialist, says, "The kids themselves
expect the school to be comfortable and calm. Problems in the
hallway are rare and can be dealt with easily because everyone
knows what should be happening."

PRACTICING FOR SUCCESS

School-wide routines, including those for hallways, are taught during the first weeks of school. Teachers go over the expected behaviors with their students, model them, and practice with their
classes. When students return from school breaks, and at other

Four Corners Demographics

✦ Setting: Public school in a small city in the Northeast

✦ Number of students: 245

✦ Grades: PreK to 5

✦ Number of staff: 49

✦ Languages spoken by students: English, Russian, Moldovan, Spanish,
Urdu

times throughout the year, there might be refresher sessions. "The key is to keep practicing all year," says first grade teacher Betsy Godin Conz.

It also helps to have a common school-wide signal for quiet (two fingers raised in a "V" at Four Corners). Such a shared signal gives everyone a way to remind each other about hallway behavior. One second grader says, "It can be sometimes hard to be quiet in the hallway, but you have to be because other people are learning. But sometimes people can't help it and they talk. Then you have to put up the quiet signal because they forgot what to do or maybe didn't know."

Establishing clear expectations for hallway behavior benefits the whole school environment at Four Corners. "It's just one of the routines that the school has established to foster an environment where teaching and learning are respected," says principal Gail Healy.

FROM THE WINTER 2005 ISSUE OF THE *RESPONSIVE CLASSROOM* NEWSLETTER.

Hallway Greeters

Welcoming adults ease the morning transition

BY SADIE FISCHESSER

NEFC STAFF MEMBER

When the morning bell rings, Linda Stephenson, the guidance counselor at Dame School, steps out of her office. A moment later, children start coming through the front door of the school. "Good morning, Parker," Linda says to one first grader. As children walk into the building and start down the long corridors that lead to the classrooms, they pass Linda and several other adults. Some of them respond to the adults' greetings with a cheerful "Good morning!" Others return a quiet nod, rush over for a quick hug, or share a brief conversation about what happened at their house last night.

In just a couple of minutes, the flow of students has reduced to a trickle and another bell sounds to start the day. The trek through the hallway was a calm, welcoming transition to a day of learning.

A TEAM-CRAFTED SOLUTION

The hallways at Dame School used to look much different. Children would enter the building haphazardly and then talk loudly and run down the halls. This unruly and potentially unsafe transition from playground to classroom frustrated and worried the staff. "You could just feel the tension in this place, from the start of the day to the end," says first grade teacher Dawn Morris.

Staff members expressed their concern to the Dame Leadership Team, which consists of school administration, teachers and support staff, members of the surrounding community, and parents. Together, the leadership team thought about proactive ways to smooth the morning transition from outside to inside. The goal was to achieve a pleasant atmosphere by helping children maintain self-control as they traveled through the long hallways.

The first step was teaching the children how safe, friendly hallway behavior looks, feels, and sounds. Teachers discussed the ideas with their students, modeled the hallway behavior they were looking for, and then let the children practice.

As the children were learning, so were all of the adults in the school community. From doing Morning Meeting in their classrooms, leadership team members were aware of the power of greetings to help children and adults establish a calm, respectful, and joyful basis for working together. They thought that greetings might have the same good effect in the hallways. Therefore, the leadership team decided to ask adults to be in the hallway greeting children as they entered the building in the morning.

LEARNING TO BE HALLWAY GREETERS

Hallway greeters were asked to look at the children as they entered the building, greet as many children as possible by name, and remind children who were off track about what walking through the hallway should look and sound like. "It's very different from hallway monitoring," explains principal Ed Barnwell, "because monitors watch, but don't engage, and they usually focus on punishment for misbehavior. We know you can't punish kids into learning social skills."

During the staff's first year of trying out their roles as hallway greeters, they needed to do a little adjusting. "We noticed that staff were clumping up in certain areas," remembers Ed. In response, the leadership team asked support staff to station themselves in certain areas and classroom teachers to be at their doors to greet and welcome children.

Now, any adult who is available acts as a hallway greeter, and the practice is much less formal. It's just part of the routine at Dame School.

Dame School Demographics

◆ Setting: Public school in a small city in the Northeast

◆ Number of students: 350

◆ Grades: PreK to 2

◆ Percentage of students eligible for free or reduced-price lunch: 40%

◆ Number of full-time staff: 30

HAPPIER HALLWAYS

"Things are much slower and happier," says Pat Steiner, the Student Support Room program assistant, when describing how things have changed. The number of students running through the hallways has decreased, and the noise level has dropped considerably.

Another significant benefit of having hallway greeters is that this simple practice gives adults and children a chance to interact in an unstructured, noninstructional setting. Through their greetings, adults make it a point to convey excitement about the day, especially with children who may have struggled with self-control the day before. The cheerful adult greetings remind these children that this is a new day and encourage them to keep trying. "It lets the children know that we really care about them, want to get to know them, and are ready to help them do their best," says Linda.

"The real change," notes Ed, "is that now the kids are initiating greetings and conversations. Children ask adults how their evening was, or how they're feeling that day. It's really amazing to see small children taking an interest in adults' lives. And it speaks to the kind of community we're building at Dame."

FROM THE NOVEMBER 2005 ISSUE OF THE *RESPONSIVE CLASSROOM* NEWSLETTER.

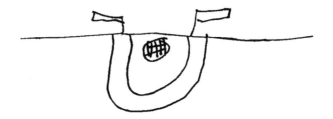

The Bathroom Opportunity

BY RUTH SIDNEY CHARNEY

NEFC CO–FOUNDER AND *RESPONSIVE CLASSROOM* CONSULTING TEACHER

In my school, the bathrooms are outside the classrooms. We make a deliberate choice not to line groups up and toilet en masse, but rather to teach children to take themselves out of the room, cross the hall, and return to their classrooms safely.

In the Primary room Jamie is working on his block building when he realizes he has to pee. Trotting over to the door, he takes a red "Boys Bathroom" card off its hook, fishes in a basket until he finds his nametag, and deftly puts it on the hook. In another moment, he is out the door and down the hall, his small five-year-old self confidently pushing the large bathroom door ajar. When he returns he pauses by the hooks, as if to do something, but then he spies something in the blocks area and heads back to continue his work-in-progress. Minutes later when Freddy goes to take himself to the bathroom, he spots Jamie's name on the hook where "Boys Bathroom" should be. Scanning the room, Freddie sees Jamie. He speaks to Jamie and together they return the bathroom card to its proper spot. All is set right.

This routine looks so simple that it would be easy to overlook much of the learning going on. Jamie is learning to recognize, perhaps read, signs. He differentiates his name from all the others and distinguishes the boys' card from the girls'. Freddie reads his name and Jamie's name. Both have learned a sequence of steps in the routine. They can notice and fix mistakes in a way that allows them to take care of themselves and someone else.

The necessity of going to the bathroom provides an opportunity for children to learn to take care of themselves outside the boundaries of the classroom, away from the supervision of the teacher. Each time students go to the bathroom, come back promptly, and resume their place in the activity of the classroom, they are practicing using their own controls and their own judgments. Along the way, they learn about responsibility and accountability—lessons they will need if they are to grow up safe and make productive choices.

We begin teaching lessons about proper bathroom use during the first six weeks of school, and we reinforce them throughout the year. Here are the steps we follow.

Step One: We have each child make a nametag

On Day One—the first day of school—the children make their nametags. They color in their names with bright colors, decorate them, and add something special that shows what they love to do. The decorations ensure that the children know their tags. Teachers use the tags to play many recognition games with the group. "Whose name am I holding now?" the teacher may ask.

**Step Two: We teach each step of the procedure for going
to the bathroom**

The teacher shows the children the bathroom. She has them practice pushing open the door, pulling the toilet paper out properly,
using the flusher. She models taking off the bathroom card, putting
up her nametag, even leaving the room and returning. She invites
the children to practice all these steps.

**Step Three: We make sure that children understand
the reasons for and significance of our routines**

"Why is it important that you remember to put your nametag up
on the hook when you go to the bathroom?" the teacher asks the
children. They talk about safety. She explains that she needs to
know where they are at all times. "My job," she tells them, "is to
make sure I know where you are and that you are safe. Your job
is to help me by letting me know when you go to the bathroom."

"How do I know that you are in the bathroom?" the teacher asks.

"Because," says Juana, "you see our names on the hook."

The teacher nods. "What does that tell me?" she asks.

"That we are in the bathroom," the children reply.

In this short interchange a contract based on mutual trust is being
established. The children gain trust from the knowledge that the
teacher will keep them safe in school. The teacher creates trust by
offering her students the privilege of sharing in their care.

**Step Four: We anticipate and are ready to deal with mistakes
and limit-testing**

I employ logical consequences that help children look at the choices
they make when they don't follow through on the expectations. I

think of logical consequences as action plans that help us to spot the unacceptable behavior, to try and fix the things that we broke, to figure out ways to improve in the future so that we can earn back our trust and privileges and regain original responsibilities.

LEARNING FROM MISTAKES: THE BATHROOM MESS IN SECOND GRADE

The problem

One spring we realized that children were deliberately making messes in the bathroom. We saw puddles on the floor where puddles need not be, floating globs in the basins, doodles on the walls. Although the younger classes shared the bathroom, it seemed more likely the "work" of the second graders.

Bringing the problem to the children

The teacher and principal met with the entire second grade class. The teacher explained that there was a problem that needed to be solved by everyone. Describing what she had observed, she noted the messes in the bathroom and the work that it made for the custodian. It had to stop, she informed the children. While they figured out what to do, students would have to ask the teacher when they needed to use the bathroom, at least for now.

"Has anyone else noticed some mess-ups in the bathroom?" she asked. There was no reluctance to contribute. The teacher was careful to keep a keen distinction between things and people. She was drawing attention to the acts, not the people.

"Why do you think that might bother your teachers and your principal?" she asked. The children easily added their observations and responses to the problem. It was clear that even the children who might have perpetrated the mess were contributing.

The teacher also asked why sometimes we do things like that and offered an example of a time she flooded the bathtub at home and caused water to leak down into the kitchen on her parents' heads! There was general laughter. Many contributions centered around the notion of "fun" rather than "bad." One student suggested that if you were feeling frustrated with your work, you might want to go into the bathroom and throw stuff around. The responses were acknowledged by the staff, validated, and accepted. It was particularly striking when a shy child suggested quietly that sometimes you do have accidents and it is "really really embarrassing to admit it. It's so embarrassing that you don't tell anyone." Classmates nodded agreement.

"What can we do about being embarrassed to ask for help to clean up an accident?" the teacher asked. "Teachers need to understand and not get too mad," someone said. "Yeah," others agreed, "even if you forget."

The discussion also focused on the reasons to take care of the bathroom, the need to share in its care and upkeep. The teacher and principal wanted to reinforce the concept that bathroom care was their community responsibility. The children participated in a powerful conversation about the reasons to take care of their space, to consider others' feelings, to recognize the work of cleaning up a mess, to find different ways to take out frustrations.

AN ACTION PLAN

The children were sent off to construct three rules for bathroom care. Their spirit was serious and thoughtful. By the end of this process, the bathroom had become "our bathroom" and the task a challenge about issues of respect. One of the final rules was, "Tell the teacher if you had an accident. Teachers shouldn't get very angry if you forgot."

The rules were written on a decorated sign and posted in the bathroom. Students read the rules aloud to the younger groups. The custodian was invited to a meeting and helped the children arrange a "cleanup bucket," just in case there were those accidents.

With the rules now on the wall, the class felt that they were ready to hang their bathroom passes back on the hook. They were ready to take better care of their bathroom. They understood that if they forgot, the teacher would again take charge of the passes and that they would not be responsible for their own selves. And that, as one student said, would be a "wicked drag."

WORTH THE TIME

Of course, even after modeling, practice, and many successful trips to the bathroom, children will have lapses that fit their developmental stage. Six-year-old boys may attempt a mad dash into the girls' bathroom. Six-year-old girls come back giggling or in a snit to expose this outrage. Eight-year-olds need reminders that bathrooming is not a social event—"You do not need to go to the bathroom every time a friend needs to go." Many ten-year-olds also love to congregate for social purposes, to tell secrets or gossip out of sight of the teacher (they hope). Restless students make numerous forays, especially when the classroom subject matter befuddles them. Graffiti and petty vandalism are common bathroom misdemeanors.

Given that such lapses are inevitable, it may seem easier, although terribly time-consuming, to take children to the bathroom. Many schools still require this. It avoids hassles and problems. Or does it? I strongly contend that the routines of our classrooms must be used as opportunities to teach decent behavior, not to constrict it.

So with our students, we practice going to the bathroom, walking down the halls, first together and then in pairs. We teach them to put up a name card on a "Bathroom Out" hook and to remember to remove the card when they return. We are prepared to rein-force and remind, because if students "forget" the rules or choose not to follow them, they may lose the privilege of going to the bathroom on their own—at least until they are ready to show that they remember and choose to follow the class rules.

I firmly believe that the time we spend is well worth the result we get: children who are developing a sense of autonomy and self-control, who know how to manage themselves outside the classroom—even when the teacher isn't watching.

FROM THE *RESPONSIVE CLASSROOM* WEBSITE

WWW.RESPONSIVECLASSROOM.ORG, FIRST POSTED ON JULY 1, 1999.

Recess and Lunch

New Ways to Play

Improving the quality of recess

BY NEVADA BROMLEY

FREELANCE EDUCATIONAL WRITER

Many of us hold memories of recess as twenty minutes of liberation, twice a day. Twenty glorious minutes of running like the wind, teeter-tottering, swinging, chatting with friends. A chance to let loose and relax. Yet, we also remember it as a place of tribulation, a place where the balance of power was continually tested and defined, and virtually no guidance was offered from the nearby adults. Often, the conflicts that erupted on the playground were continued in the classroom, so students had difficulty turning their attention back to academics.

Sadly, rather than confronting the problems of recess, many elementary schools today are choosing to reduce or even eliminate it. They see recess as a waste of minutes that could be better spent on academics or as an awkward block of time that compromises the off-duty time granted in teacher contracts. In some new schools, lack of space is another rationale for eliminating recess, and play-grounds are not even part of the building plan.

Fortunately, many other educators are taking the opposite approach. These educators believe that recess can greatly enhance children's ability to concentrate on academics by giving them a much-needed break and allowing them to release physical energy. In addition, they see recess as rich with opportunities for learning and practicing social skills. Recognizing the vital role that recess can play in children's physical, social, and cognitive development, these schools are working to maximize the potential of recess by changing its structure.

INTENTIONALLY TEACHING RECESS

Chip Wood, co-founder of Northeast Foundation for Children and a strong advocate for keeping recess alive and well in schools, has worked for the past ten years with elementary and middle schools committed to restructuring recess. Believing that "learning time is maximized in school environments where playgrounds are peace-ful, friendly, and active," Wood advocates for "teaching recess with the same intentionality with which we teach reading or math." The ultimate goal: Children will be able to play independently and cooperatively, just as they learn to read independently and work cooperatively in the classroom.

"Children have far less experience with spontaneous play outside of school now than they used to," notes Wood. "You're not as likely today to see groups of children after school playing pickup games of soccer or Kick the Can. And without these many hours of spontaneous play, how will children learn and practice the social skills, such as cooperation, conflict resolution, empathy, and responsibility, that are as essential to their survival as reading, writing, and computing?"

Olga Jarret, professor of child development at Georgia State University, asked a similar question during an interview for a *New York Times* article ("Many Schools Putting an End to Child's Play," April 7, 1998) on the decision of some schools to eliminate recess: "When do kids learn to interact with kids? We have so many latchkey kids who go home and lock the door until their parents get home. Now if they can't mingle with other kids at school or at home, how are they going to resolve conflicts with their peers?"

In his new book on school reform, *Time to Teach, Time to Learn: Changing the Pace of School* (Northeast Foundation for Children, Inc., 1999), Wood offers these recommendations to administrators and teachers working to improve the quality of recess in their schools:

✦ Before school starts in the fall, provide playground training for teachers, paraprofessionals, and others who will have important roles to play at and around recess. Then use the first two weeks of school recess to model, practice, and reinforce games, rules, and ways of playing together.

✦ Second, require that physical education teachers teach playground games as their first academic unit at the beginning of the year. Give physical education teachers supervisory authority and hold them accountable as part of their teaching duties for the nature and quality of the playground/recess experience for children. This does not mean daily recess duty. Instead, it means recognizing their professional status by making them part of the administrative team of the school. It may also mean reducing the hours the head physical education teacher spends with individual classes so she can train paraprofessionals and supervise the recess program.

✦ Finally, if at all possible, restructure the middle of the day so that recess comes before, rather than after, lunch. It makes more

sense that children would first work up an appetite through exercise and then come in to eat rather than the other way around. In many schools, the midday schedule allows for recess, then lunch, then quiet time. Teachers report that this structure works wells and helps children to be more productive and engaged in the afternoon.

SCHOOLS SEEING POSITIVE RESULTS

Schools that have taken these recommendations to heart have seen many positive results. Improvements range from far fewer playground discipline referrals and injury reports from the nurse's office to an increase in cooperative play and, ultimately, more time for academic learning.

At the Regional Multicultural Magnet School in New London, Connecticut, for example, teachers have become involved in introducing and supervising recess. Mark Farnsworth, a physical education teacher at this school, begins each school year by "teaching"

recess to students and teachers. In the fall, he teaches students and teachers how to use the recess space and equipment and introduces a wide range of recess games and activities. Throughout the year, instructional assistants, serving as designated "play leaders," facilitate student- or teacher-led activities at every recess. Although students have the option of playing independently, many choose to participate in the planned activities.

Similarly, at Coleytown Elementary School in Westport, Connecticut, physical education teachers Gina Forberg, Jennifer Rasmussen, and Lori Buskey have collaborated to make recess safer and more peaceful by teaching students how to use the playground and structuring games and activities. Recess here is primarily led by teachers' aides, with support from classroom teachers, specialty teachers, and physical education teachers.

In the fall, adults structure most of the play at Coleytown. As the year progresses, children play games more independently. K–2 students are offered options such as tag games, hopscotch, hula hoops, jump rope, and using the play structure. Children in grades

3–5 often play Capture the Flag, rounders, soccer, ball games, and jump rope. Some children do elect to walk around or read, but most participate in the structured activities. Buskey points out that "all children feel safe in knowing there is always an adult close by, someone who will step in and help if they're having a hard time resolving a conflict."

Providing more structured activities and having adults available to help children resolve conflicts during recess also has had a positive effect in Fitchburg, Massachusetts. Several schools there have instituted recess initiatives similar to those just described—and with positive results. Bonnie Baer-Simahk, Fitchburg's early childhood coordinator and the parent of a child at the J.R. Briggs School in nearby Ashburnham, has seen the benefits of physical education teacher Bob Weeks's efforts to teach children cooperative sports and games. "There's a difference in the quality of play at these schools during outdoor time, and I've seen this transferring from the school to the community playground near my home, where children of different ages play together. The kids have started to do a lot of pickup games on their own," says Baer-Simahk.

Mark Farnsworth notes that the restructuring of recess is a work in progress. Initially, the response of many teachers was "What, something else to fit into our day?" But now that teachers are experiencing the positive results, they're receptive to the changes. "There are fewer problems that occur at recess and carry over into the classroom," says Farnsworth, "which translates to more usable teaching time after recess."

FROM THE WINTER 2000 ISSUE OF THE *RESPONSIVE CLASSROOM* NEWSLETTER.

The Middle of the Day

BY GAIL HEALY

PRINCIPAL AT FOUR CORNERS ELEMENTARY SCHOOL, GREENFIELD, MASSACHUSETTS

It's a cool, crisp, autumn morning as 100 second and third graders burst onto the playground for a much-needed break from the academic demands of the day. Some make a beeline to a kickball game starting up in a far corner of the playground with the "recess/lunch teacher" serving as pitcher and referee. Others dart to the play structure supervised by an instructional aide. In mid-field, a lively round of relay races starts to take shape with the help of two fifth-grade peer mediators. In yet another corner of the field, a game of Cut the Cake, led by a special education teacher, quickly grows from a group of three to a group of twenty-three. Children move in and out of games with ease. There are no lengthy debates about rules, no fights about who can play, no tears. There are no children wandering aimlessly about, and for those who prefer a quieter break in the day, there is a supply of books, paper, and markers under a nearby maple tree. It's an active, playful, and peaceful twenty-five minutes, and children and adults leave it feeling refreshed and relaxed.

This scenario may sound too good to be true, but it's actually a fairly typical fall recess at our school. It's the result of a concerted effort that began two years ago to address the recurring conflicts and tensions that surfaced daily during recess and lunch.

During previous years, we had worked hard as a whole staff to improve the learning climate in our school. Although we had made great strides, one part of the day—the midday recess/lunchtime—remained problematic.

Not only was recess filled with conflicts that inevitably made their way back into the classroom, but many students simply had no idea what to do during this time. Hesitant to join one of the highly competitive and physical games that typically dominated recess, they wandered aimlessly around the playground, interacting with no one. The resulting feelings of alienation often led to conflicts later in the day.

Lunchtime was not much better. It was noisy and chaotic and filled with mishaps. Children often felt excluded, and there was a glaring lack of consistency between the expectations in the classroom and those in the lunchroom.

Adults were spending far too much time writing and sending home discipline notes, and everyone—teachers, parents, and students—felt frustrated. Our staff decided that it was time to confront the problems. Here's how we approached them.

PHASE ONE: GETTING STARTED

During the first year, we reflected on the problems, explored possible solutions, and took a few initial steps toward improving recess and lunch.

Reordering the middle of the day

One of the first changes we made was to reverse the order of recess and lunch so that children went outside and played before coming inside to eat. In his book *Time to Teach, Time to Learn: Changing the Pace of School* (Northeast Foundation for Children, Inc., 1999), Chip Wood, Northeast Foundation for Children co-founder, urges schools to make this change because of his belief that eating first and then going out to play is "disruptive to both the educational system and the digestive system. Better to work up an appetite with exercise, come in to eat, settle down, and take a rest."

After making this change for two out of the three recess/lunch periods (schedule constraints prevented changing the third), teachers immediately noticed a positive change in students' emotions and demeanor when they reentered the classroom after lunch. Also, there were fewer conflicts in the lunchroom and on the playground, and those that occurred were mediated more quickly.

Improving K–1 recess first

At the same time, we began having whole-staff brainstorms about recess and lunch: How could we structure recess to make it more enjoyable and safe for all students? How could we make lunch calmer and more relaxing for everyone?

As a first step, we decided to focus on improving the kindergarten/first grade recess. The plan was to increase the number of adults on the playground and to give them more active roles.

Previously there were two adults on the playground, and their involvement was limited to intervening when problems arose. Now there would be four adults and each one would lead a different game or activity that students would be required either to participate in or to watch.

We didn't have the funds to hire two additional staff members for recess, but we were able to change our schedules so that two instructional aides could be at recess in addition to the two paraprofessionals already there. I also made an effort to be there whenever possible, as did the behavior management teacher. After trying this plan for a few weeks, we saw such a dramatic improvement in the quality of play and social interactions that we knew we were on the right track.

PHASE TWO: TAKING IT TO ALL GRADES

Encouraged by these early successes and eager for more widespread improvements, I made contact over the summer with all the adults who would be involved with recess and lunch. I shared my excitement about further improving this time of the day and invited their input. This group met before school began to solidify plans and to prepare for the first days of school. Here are the key ideas we set into motion at the beginning of the year.

A change in title

We felt it was important to change the titles of certain members of the group from "paraprofessionals" to "recess/lunch teachers." This title more accurately reflected their role and our belief that, in the words of Chip Wood, "teaching recess and lunch is just as important as teaching reading and math." Additional members of the group, including the behavior management teacher and several instructional aides, began to see themselves as "recess/lunch teachers" during the middle of the day.

Teaching games

In the first week of school, recess/lunch teachers were paired with individual classes, grades K-5, during recess. The adults taught one game a day. We chose games that encouraged cooperation and could be played independently by the students. Every student was expected either to participate actively or to keenly observe the games.

During this stage, I received several phone calls from concerned parents who wondered why their child "didn't have recess anymore" or "had to play a game during recess."

I addressed these concerns as they arose and also included information in our September and October parent newsletters explaining our rationale and plans for teaching recess and lunch. For the most part, families were very supportive of this new approach.

Opening the play structure

At the same time that games were being taught on the playground, we were teaching individual classes how to use and care for the play structure.

At the start of the school year, the play structure was wrapped in orange construction tape with a large CLOSED sign hanging in the center. Each day a different class was chosen to do an exploration of the structure led by one of the recess/lunch teachers. Each part of the structure was explored and its potential uses discussed, demonstrated, and practiced. Rules for safety were talked about, written up, and sent to every staff member and classroom. The structure was opened once every class had gone through this experience.

Teaching lunch

During the first four days of school, classroom teachers accompanied their classes to the cafeteria in the morning to practice lunch. Several recess/lunch teachers, including me, were present to explain and model everything from lunchroom procedures—such as where to go to get your lunch, what to take when you get there, what to do if you forget something—to table manners, including where and how to sit at tables and what you might want to talk about. Not only did children enjoy this modeling, but it also made an immediate positive impact on their behavior at lunch.

Reflecting and revising

Then, every Friday, the recess/lunch team met to talk about how things were going and to make changes as needed. Did the children need more supervision? Less supervision? Although our ultimate goal was for the children to increase their independence during recess and lunch, we were careful not to pull out support too soon.

By the end of the second week of school, we all agreed that the fourth/fifth grade recess was running smoothly. Adults were still involved in the games, but the children were for the most part organizing their own games and doing so in a friendly and inclusive way.

Several weeks later, we felt that the second/third grade recess was also ready for more independence. We began by offering them a "choice" day on Fridays when children practiced leading games and had access to recess equipment such as jump ropes and balls. Student mediators, who had been participating in the games up to this point, were now being asked to lead them. Meanwhile, we decided not to make any changes in the kindergarten/first grade recess for the time being. The high degree of adult involvement still seemed essential for this younger group.

Now, many people notice that lunch is calmer and recess more peaceful this year. Teachers comment on the greater consistency in the rules throughout the school. Perhaps most importantly, children seem more relaxed during recess and lunch. Because of this, the middle of the day truly does offer a break from the demands of academics. It's a time for children to rest and recharge. When they return to the classroom, they are ready to learn. It has taken a strong team effort to reach this point, an effort that everyone agrees has been well worth the time and energy.

FROM THE WINTER 2001 ISSUE OF THE *RESPONSIVE CLASSROOM* NEWSLETTER.

Communicating
about Lunch

BY SADIE FISCHESSER
NEFC STAFF MEMBER

("They're fine when they're with me. But when they step outside the walls of my classroom, their behavior falls apart," says a fifth grade teacher. It's a common lament. Many teachers succeed in teaching children to be calm and respectful in the classroom, only to have the children "lose it" in other areas of the school building.

That was the case at Kensington Avenue School in Springfield, Massachusetts, where teachers began using the *Responsive Classroom* approach about a decade ago. Although the children's classroom behavior improved, their behavior elsewhere in the school remained largely unchanged. The difference was most noticeable in the lunchrooms, tight spaces where sound echoed easily. The noise made it even more difficult for students to maintain self-control.

To address the problem, a committee of teachers, other staff, and parents met and decided to offer professional development to the lunch staff, or "lunch teachers," as they're called at Kensington. The goal would be to help the lunch teachers use the same communication techniques that teachers were using with students in the classrooms. The consistency, the committee reasoned, should help students carry their calm and respectful classroom behavior into the lunchrooms. Here's how the process works today.

A MINI-WORKSHOP EARLY IN THE SCHOOL YEAR

During the first six weeks of school, lunch teachers at Kensington are asked to come to school early one day for a mini-workshop. The lunch teachers—a combination of parents, paraprofessionals, and others—are compensated at their regular wage for attending.

Tina Valentine, a head teacher and a certified *Responsive Classroom* consulting teacher, leads the thirty-minute workshop. Here's what it covers:

✦ **Using the all-school signal for quiet** Kensington's agreed-upon signal is a raised hand. The lunch teachers practice using the signal. They raise their hands without adding other verbal directions (shushing or talking), hand signals (finger pointing), or facial expressions, and then they wait for quiet.

✦ **Using positive language to reinforce and redirect behavior** Tina focuses on some key phrases to use in different situations, such as "Remind me what you should be doing right now," or "I see that you're keeping your hands to yourself."

✦ **Keeping directions to students clear and simple** For example, instead of saying to a child, "You are not supposed to put your tray there. We have talked about safe stacking of trays, and the way you put your tray here is not safe. Please remove your tray and stack it the way it is supposed to be stacked," the lunch teachers are encouraged to say, "Stop. Please stack your tray on top of the others."

Lunch teachers find these communication techniques effective for expressing high expectations of students in the lunchrooms and helping students maintain self-control. Often, they say the workshop helps them feel more comfortable with children, which in turn puts the children more at ease.

FOLLOW-UP HELP

About a week after the workshop, Tina checks in with the lunch teachers to see how things are going and to identify any problems. If a lunch teacher is having trouble with something, Tina makes time to work with that teacher on the issue. If it seems that the group as a whole is struggling, she schedules a refresher with all of them.

THE BENEFITS OF CONSISTENCY

The environment in the lunchrooms has improved dramatically since the school began working with the lunch teachers in this way. Building on that success, the school began offering similar workshops and coaching, with some modifications, to the office and custodial staff. Principal Margaret Thompson notes, "You just don't hear adults raise their voices at children here." Tina adds, "Consistent language fosters a safe environment for learning in the school."

Kensington Avenue Demographics

✦ Setting: Urban public school in the Northeast

✦ Number of students: 385

✦ Grades: K to 5

✦ Number of full- and part-time staff: 44

✦ Percentage of students eligible for free or reduced-price lunch: 91%

✦ Largest ethnic group among students: Hispanic (60%)

FROM THE FALL 2004 ISSUE OF THE *RESPONSIVE CLASSROOM* NEWSLETTER.

Special Area Classrooms

Using the *Responsive Classroom*® Approach in Special Area Classrooms ✦ **54**

Getting to Know You ✦ **61**

Using the *Responsive Classroom* Approach in Special Area Classrooms

BY ALICE YANG

NEFC EDITOR/WRITER

Music teachers, art teachers, physical education teachers, librarians, and other specialists are an integral part of school. They play a role, as all staff members do, in teaching children to be responsible, caring learners. But unlike self-contained classroom teachers, specialists see hundreds of students a week, often travel to more than one school, and typically have barely an hour a week to teach each group of children.

Given these constraints, many specialists wonder how they can make time to bring social skills into the curriculum, nurture a sense of classroom community, or build meaningful relationships with and among students—all critical elements in helping children succeed academically and socially.

At Penn Valley Elementary School in Levittown, Pennsylvania, the specialists have found a way. The school has just completed its fifth year of school-wide implementation of the *Responsive Classroom* approach to creating safe, challenging, and joyful classrooms that integrate the teaching of social and academic skills. With creativity, help from each other, and support from the school administration, the specialists have brought elements of the *Responsive Classroom* strategies into their daily teaching, with positive results for the children and themselves.

"Specialists are a part of our school," says Penn Valley principal Karen Casto. "Having them use the *Responsive Classroom* practices and making sure everyone on staff is using the practices the same way gives a consistent message to children. It's good teaching practice."

THE STRATEGIES IN ACTION

One big thing that got the specialists interested in using the *Responsive Classroom* strategies was seeing an overall improvement in student behavior since Penn Valley began the school-wide implementation. "I've seen a positive change," says PE teacher Rich Hamilton, who joined the staff at Penn Valley years before it began using the approach. Children will always have their differences, he says, but now they're more willing to work through them. "I think it's a better social climate for the kids."

Today, one can see signs of the *Responsive Classroom* approach at work throughout the school.

Elements of Morning Meeting—a half-hour, whole-class gathering that begins the school day—are common. For example, art teacher Trisha Roach relies heavily on circle seating, a standard format for

Morning Meeting. Children sit in a circle for sharing—about their favorite color, what they like to draw, or a work in progress—or for introductions to new art materials or new art concepts. Librarian Carolyn Wert uses circle seating to have children share about their favorite books or authors. And in Nancy Adamczyk's music class, students regularly do Morning Meeting-style greetings and activities involving rhythmic chants or songs.

In addition, the specialists attend Morning Meetings in different self-contained classrooms throughout the year as their schedules allow. This gives them a chance to get to know children better. "I don't have as much conversation time with students as other teachers because I have 500 students," says Adamczyk. "Going to Morning Meetings lets me see kids, and lets them see me, on a different level than in music class. My being there shows my interest in what they're learning outside of music."

Other components of the *Responsive Classroom* approach have made their way into the special areas as well. Children entering library class are greeted by a written message from the librarian in the style of the *Responsive Classroom's* News and Announcements chart. "Greetings, Library Pals! Today is Thursday, …" the chart sings out on one typical day. The children sit down in front of the chart to read the message. It gives the date, mentions a few authors who were born on this day in history, offers one or two other historical tidbits, and then notes the day's lesson before ending with a brain teaser just for fun.

In another part of the building, music teacher Adamczyk has built Academic Choice into a class period for fifth graders. Academic Choice is a structured way to give children choices, within boundaries set by the teacher, about what and how they'll learn. The children are deciding whether they'll use the period to explore

rhythms or experiment with melodies. They're also planning how they'll accomplish their goals in their chosen area of learning.

Meanwhile, in the art classroom, children are busy working near a display of their hopes and dreams for the year in art. Roach helped the students create the display during the first week of school. Later in the year, she'll take some time to reflect with students on how far they've come in meeting their goals.

And in PE class, teacher Rich Hamilton is doing a Guided Discovery of a jump rope with a class of kindergartners and first graders. Guided Discovery is a *Responsive Classroom* strategy for introducing materials to students. Children are encouraged to take care of materials and to use them creatively and respectfully.

Adamczyk thinks that all these strategies have boosted children's ability to handle challenging work. "I'm able to accomplish a lot more with my classes. The kinds of activities I do with them now are not activities I could've done my first year, and I really think it's because of using the *Responsive Classroom* techniques," she says. "I'm covering more advanced musical concepts, having students create their own compositions, choose instruments, do performances."

CONSISTENCY IN CLASSROOM MANAGEMENT

One particularly important change that specialists have made is to use discipline strategies that are consistent with those used in self-contained classrooms. As Adamczyk puts it, "If there's a kind of language or certain rules that teachers are using, and I carry them over into my area, it's just going to make my classroom run more smoothly."

Accordingly, she and other specialists have adjusted their language with children. Among other things, they say "I notice that you …" or "Show me how you …" rather than "I like how you …" or "I want you to …" to reinforce the idea that children should act for their own and the group's good, rather than to please the teacher. Whenever possible, the specialist teachers also use the same signals,

such as the raised hand or a soft chime, that other teachers are using to tell children to stop what they're doing and give the teacher their attention.

The specialists also teach children that rules for behavior in their regular classroom carry over to the special areas. Early in the year, students bring a copy of their classroom rules to their special classrooms. The specialists discuss with children what it would look like to follow these rules in the special area, and some specialists post the rules in their classrooms. The message to children is clear: The same high expectations in place elsewhere in the school also apply to specials.

Often, the specialists' adoption of classroom management techniques comes out of the need to address a specific, pressing problem. Late last year, for example, a group of fifth graders were having an especially bad case of the late spring jitters, and behavior problems were showing up in the special areas.

After some brainstorming with Lynn Majewski, Penn Valley's instructional support BRIDGE teacher, the four specialists realized that part of the solution was to be consistent—among themselves and with the self-contained classroom teachers—in their use of logical consequences for rule-breaking. All four agreed to use the same progression of consequences, and the number of behavior problems soon dropped. "It helped that we were all on the same page," says Wert. Children were more able to maintain self-control when they knew that the same consequences would follow inappropriate behavior. And they were more able to regain self-control when they had the same chances to manage their composure, she says.

MORE SHARED RESPONSIBILITY

Along with more consistency, Penn Valley has seen more shared responsibility among the specialists and the self-contained classroom teachers in recent years. For example, last year Roach noticed an unusual amount of name-calling and similar hurtful behavior in one of her classes. She and the self-contained classroom teacher decided that it was time for a whole-class problem-solving meeting. Realizing that this was a joint problem that required a joint solution, the two teachers decided that they would both be present for the meeting and would co-lead it.

On the chosen day for the meeting, the classroom teacher brought the class to the art room at the usual time, and stayed. The two teachers then used the next twenty minutes to talk with the class, identifying the recent problem behavior and helping students to come up with ideas for addressing it. The ideas ranged from new seating arrangements, to ways of responding if someone calls you a name, to what bystanders can do if they witness name calling. Roach says there was a marked difference in the children's behavior after the meeting.

Looking back at the last few years, Majewski sums up the change that's taken place at Penn Valley. The special classes are now regarded more as part of the school, she says. Instead of the "You're not my teacher" mentality that many students have toward specialist teachers, children at Penn Valley view their specialists as equal members of the community of teachers, according to Majewski. Roach agrees. "Specials are seen as part of the school day," she says, "not just a time to go and play, but a time to learn."

FROM THE *RESPONSIVE CLASSROOM* WEBSITE
WWW.RESPONSIVECLASSROOM.ORG, FIRST POSTED ON JUNE 1, 2001.

Getting to Know You

*Answers from teachers for helping specialists
get to know students better*

QUESTION | *"Specials" teachers often see each child for
only one hour a week. What's one way that you and a special
area teacher have worked together to help him/her get to know
your students better?*

Margaret Berry teaches second graders at the University
School of Nashville in Tennessee.

ANSWER | At our school, we've found that fostering a culture
of regular, two-way communication helps all of us to know the
children well. For example, classroom teachers issue a standing
invitation for specials teachers to join daily Morning Meetings.
It's an easy and fun way to learn about the students. Even joining
each classroom's Morning Meeting only once can give the specialist a better perspective on students' interests and talents.

Another way we help specials teachers know the children is to post a great deal of student work throughout the school. Plus, we often communicate by email, particularly if something new happens in a child's life, such as the birth of a sibling or the death of a relative.

Our specials teachers also share information with us. One music teacher holds a Talent Day to showcase children's special abilities or interests. For example, one child did magic tricks; another shared some of her artwork. The audience of classmates, classroom teacher, and families is hugely supportive. Talent Day has become a favorite school tradition, as well as an important way for all of the teachers to know the students better.

Donna Petit teaches kindergartners and first graders at Jay/Westfield Elementary School in Jay, Vermont.

ANSWER | I've found that inviting our specials teachers to join Morning Meetings is a great way for everyone to get to know each other better. For example, once or twice a month on Wednesdays, the only days when our PE teacher Pat D'Pietro is in our building, she joins our Morning Meeting as one of the sharers. This offers us a chance to get to know her not just as our PE teacher, but also as a "real" person. Once we learned that she has a garden and loves to grow vegetables. Another time we learned that she hiked up nearby Wheeler Mountain. Listening to the other sharings of the day also lets Pat learn about the children. And the questions and comments following the sharings open the door to further conversations later in the day. As a further way of connecting, Pat invites two students to share with me, after each PE class, what she and the children did that day.

As the year goes on, Pat sometimes brings in new greetings or activities to teach us. Having her join us on Wednesdays is something we all look forward to.

Tracey Gordon teaches fifth and sixth graders at Cambridgeport School in Cambridge, Massachusetts.

ANSWER | I've had great success co-teaching lessons with specialists. Last year, I worked with Gina, our technology specialist, to create a mini-unit for our study of 18th and 19th century American Indian cultures. During the planning, I shared my insight into specific students and the ways they learned best.

Although I supplemented and supported Gina, she did most of the teaching. She began by inviting the students to share their ideas of what characteristics make an effective leader. Next, she helped them explore how certain Western tribes chose their leaders. After a brainstorm and webbing exercise using the "Inspiration®" computer program, the children each claimed a word that described one quality of a leader. They created a unique hand-drawn symbol for that quality, and Gina taught them how to scan their symbols into the computer and print them onto transferable, iron-on paper. Finally, students ironed their symbols onto a large "power shirt" that we hung in the classroom.

Co-teaching this mini-unit enabled Gina to know the students better. It also enabled the students to know her better. As an added benefit, the children got to see two teachers working together— a useful model for their own collaborative projects.

FROM THE NOVEMBER 2005 ISSUE OF THE *RESPONSIVE CLASSROOM* NEWSLETTER.

Building
Community

All-School Meetings

Coming together as a community

BY SADIE FISCHESSER

NEFC STAFF MEMBER

In a school with over 500 students and more than eighty staff, getting to know one another can be difficult. At K.T. Murphy Elementary School in Stamford, Connecticut, the staff and administrators addressed this by creating an all-school meeting format that uses the structure of Morning Meeting.

Every month, all members of the school—including many parents—join for a meeting led by students. From month to month, different grades take the lead. At one typical meeting in late winter, the first graders are leading. After a group of students welcomes everyone, one child takes the microphone to review the pre-arranged Greeting for the day, in which each grade will represent a different insect. This Greeting was chosen because the first graders had been studying insects in science. Every class in the school has practiced the Greeting before this gathering.

"Good morning, everyone," say the first graders this morning, as they all make big biting motions in the air to represent mosquitoes. Around the room gestures of stinging and flying accompany other greetings.

Next, more first graders get up to lead the Sharing. They call up each grade to talk about what they have learned in science. Groups from each grade explain posters and projects they're working on; some share in both English and Spanish.

After the Sharing, another class of first graders steps forward to lead the Group Activity. Continuing with the insect theme, the activity is a variation of "Head, shoulders, knees, and toes," only the words are "Head, thorax, abdomen, wing." Immediately the room erupts with children and adults singing, flapping their arms, and making antennae over their heads.

Finally, a set of first graders leads the News and Announcements. They use an overhead projector to show the chart so that everyone can read along.

Before the meeting ends, a drawing decides which grade will lead the next month's meeting. "Kids can't wait to see who's next to lead," says Kim Moore, a first grade teacher. With 500 children beating out a drum roll on the floor, the student leaders draw an envelope. When the leaders are announced, the students pass to the winning class a shield with each component of Morning Meeting represented on it.

CAREFUL PREPARATION

To enable the careful preparation required for these meetings to be successful, guest teachers provide substitute coverage while the grade level teachers meet to make initial plans. The teachers then

Morning Meeting
at a Glance

Morning Meeting, a key component of the *Responsive Classroom* approach to teaching, is a powerful tool for building community and integrating the teaching of social and academic skills. Every day, for around thirty minutes first thing in the morning, teachers and students gather in a circle to greet one another, share news, practice academic and social skills, and prepare for the day ahead.

The meeting consists of four components done in the order shown here:

1 Greeting Students greet each other by name. Greeting activities include handshaking, singing, clapping, and greeting in different languages.

2 Sharing Students share information about important events in their lives. Listeners offer empathic comments or ask clarifying questions.

3 Group Activity All participate in a brief, lively activity that fosters group cohesion (for example, reciting a poem, dancing, singing, or playing a game that reinforces social or academic skills).

4 News and Announcements Children read the News and Announcements chart that their teacher has written. The chart often includes an interactive activity and helps children focus on the work of the day ahead.

meet with the students to finalize details and send out an agenda to other teachers before the meeting. If necessary, student leaders visit classrooms throughout the school to teach the Greeting and the activity they're planning for the all-school meeting.

THE WHOLE SCHOOL AS A COMMUNITY

Just like Morning Meeting, which happens in every classroom at K.T. Murphy every day, these all-school meetings help students and teachers build a sense of community. "Kids get to see other kids, teachers, staff, and parents, and these people become familiar to them," says third grade teacher and *Responsive Classroom* consulting teacher Toni D'Agostino. "It really makes the school a safer place." Principal Kathy Pfister adds, "It helps us to know who we are and where we're headed together."

K.T. Murphy Demographics

+ Setting: Public school in a mid-size city in the Northeast

+ Number of students: 530

+ Grades: K to 5

+ Number of full-time teachers: 42

+ Number of total staff: 84

+ Percentage of students eligible for free or reduced-price lunch: 50%

+ Percentage of students who are non-native English speakers: 38%

FROM THE SUMMER 2004 ISSUE OF THE *RESPONSIVE CLASSROOM* NEWSLETTER.

Morning Meeting Begins at 7:15 PM!

*Ideas for using this familiar classroom routine
at back-to-school nights, open houses,
and other parent meetings*

BY PAMELA PORTER

RESPONSIVE CLASSROOM CONSULTING TEACHER

I t's back-to-school night at Flanders Elementary School in East
Lyme, Connecticut. As parents and guardians arrive at Andy
Dousis's fourth grade classroom, he welcomes them warmly
and invites them to read the News and Announcements chart
that is addressed to them.

Once most of the adults have arrived and have had a chance to
make nametags and introduce themselves to someone, Mr. Dousis
rings a chime to get the group's attention. "It's time to come to

meeting," he says, and invites everyone to find a seat in a large circle of chairs he has arranged for them.

"I'm Andy Dousis, your student's teacher," he begins. "Thank you for coming. Tonight I want to share some of the things we'll be learning in school this year and to give us all a chance to get to know each other a little better. We start every day in this classroom with a twenty- to thirty-minute Morning Meeting. Tonight we'll do our own version of a Morning Meeting so you can experience firsthand what this meeting is like."

Teachers using the *Responsive Classroom* approach often structure family nights around a Morning Meeting format. This sets a positive tone for the evening, helps adults to feel welcomed and included, and gives families a firsthand experience of something their children do every day at school.

Whether it's back-to-school night or one of the curriculum meetings her school holds each year for parents and guardians, Sarah Magee, a special education teacher at Regional Multicultural Magnet School in New London, Connecticut, says she always begins these evenings in a circle and uses a Morning Meeting format.

"It helps develop positive community relationships," she notes, "and it lets families experience something their children take part in every day. After adults go through a Morning Meeting, they come to understand the importance of teaching social skills, and they see how academic and social learning are woven together during this part of the day."

GOALS FOR THE MEETING

When planning a Morning Meeting for parents and guardians, keep in mind the following two goals:

1 *To foster a sense of community and help people get to know each other.* One important goal for these evenings is to set a friendly, welcoming tone that helps people feel at ease and included as members of the school community. We know that when children feel that they belong, they participate in more meaningful ways. This is true for adults as well. Teachers report that when parents and guardians know and feel comfortable with the school staff and with one another, they are more likely to get their children together outside of school, volunteer, participate actively in the life of the school, and seek help for their children when it's needed.

2 *To share information about the classroom and curriculum in ways that are interactive, meaningful, and fun.* The meeting can be used as an effective starting point for sharing information about the curriculum and events in the classroom. But more importantly, when parents/guardians experience a Morning Meeting— exchanging greetings, learning each other's names, engaging in an activity together—they see for themselves the powerful social and academic learning that happens at these meetings and the value of taking time to build a sense of classroom community.

GUIDELINES FOR LEADING A MORNING MEETING WITH PARENTS AND GUARDIANS

One of the most important things to keep in mind is that some adults may feel awkward and unsure of what to do when they first enter the classroom. They may feel they have already taken a big risk in just coming for the meeting. Be sure to greet people at the door when they arrive. Provide nametags so people can learn and become comfortable using each other's names. And have a message chart and a meeting circle ready and waiting for them.

September 23

Welcome, Families and Friends.

Please come in and make a nametag. Take a look around the room. Then find one person you don't know well and introduce yourself.

On the chart, please write one question or comment you have about what your child will be doing this year.

We will begin at 7:15.

Mr. Dousis

Once the adults are gathered in the circle, introduce the meeting. It's usually sufficient to say that the students begin every day with a Morning Meeting—a twenty- to thirty-minute routine that builds community, sets a positive tone for the day, nurtures confidence and excitement about learning, and improves academic and social skills—and that tonight the adults will have a chance to experience a Morning Meeting firsthand. Here are some additional guidelines for making the meeting successful.

Choose low-risk activities that help people get to know each other or that connect with the curriculum

Especially at the beginning of the year, avoid Greetings and Activities that are too silly or require physical contact. It's also important to avoid activities that could embarrass anyone or put an individual on the spot. A Greeting in which two adults are partnered and then introduce each other to the group often works well: "This is Magda and her son is Issac. He loves basketball."

Group activities that work well in this setting include "A Warm Wind Blows" and "I'm Thinking of a Number Between 1 and 100." Both activities keep the focus on the group as a whole and are easy to teach and fun to play.

You may also ask students for suggestions of an appropriate activity for their families. Family members often enjoy learning a favorite activity of the students.

If you include Sharing, keep it brief and focused. For example, you might ask people to share the names and grades of their children or one thing their child likes to do. A round robin format lets everyone say something (or pass) but does not require questions and comments. This saves time and avoids the lengthy introduction and teaching that other forms of sharing require.

Bring the chart into the circle and use it to launch into the discussion of curriculum

Just as it's used in the classroom, the News and Announcements chart can be used to shift the focus to the topic at hand. For example, the interactive element on the chart might be "Write one question you have about what your child will be doing this year." Reading the parents' and guardians' questions provides a nice segue into the topic for the evening.

Teachers may also want to share a sample of a News and Announcements chart from the classroom. Through looking at a chart that the students and teacher have already worked with, the group will see the wide range of academic skills addressed in this component of Morning Meeting.

Before moving on to the topic for the evening, take a few minutes to reflect together on the meeting

After the meeting, it can be valuable to ask everyone to reflect briefly on the experience. Here are some simple questions:

✦ How do you feel now compared with when you first entered the room?

✦ What social skills did we practice in the meeting? What academic skills?

✦ What are some of the ways Morning Meeting might help children feel comfortable, confident, and ready for learning?

Dear Parents and Guardians,

There's a wonderful new beginning to your child's school day! It's called Morning Meeting, and it's a great way to build community, set a positive tone, increase excitement about learning, and improve academic and social skills.

Morning Meeting usually takes between twenty and thirty minutes. First thing each morning, the children and I gather in a circle. We begin by greeting each other. Every day, your child hears his or her name spoken by a classmate in a friendly and cheerful manner.

Next, a few students share some interesting news, followed by a conversation with the class. This helps students listen carefully, think about what they hear, formulate good questions, and learn about each other. When your child shares, s/he'll have a chance to feel that his/her ideas are valued and that the other children care.

After sharing, there is an activity for the whole class. We might sing or recite a poem or play a math game. The activity time helps the class feel united as a group, reinforces academic skills, and helps the children learn how to cooperate and solve problems.

Finally, we read the News and Announcements chart, which helps students think about the day ahead. Sometimes, I use this time to teach a reading, punctuation, or math skill.

Morning Meeting lets children know every day that school is a safe place where everyone's feelings and ideas are important. We'd love to have you visit a Morning Meeting. Just give me a call to arrange a good time. You'll see for yourself why we're all so excited about this start to our day.

Sincerely,

Follow up with written information about Morning Meeting

Because some family members will be unable to attend school gatherings, it's a good idea to write up information about Morning Meeting and other topics that you plan to address at this special evening session so that this information can be sent to absent families. See the box for an example of a letter to a child's home.

Some teachers also follow up with regular newsletters to families. Along with updates about what's going on in math, writing, science, and social studies, fourth grade teacher Mike Anderson includes a section on Morning Meeting in his weekly newsletter. Here's one example:

"This week during the Sharing portion of our meeting, we're continuing to work on creating a good lead for narrative writing. We've also enjoyed using the Group Activity time to reenact scenes from the book I'm reading aloud. In addition to helping students learn to cooperate and work as a team, this activity has strengthened students' comprehension of key scenes of the book."

MULTIPLE BENEFITS

Since Andy Dousis began holding Morning Meetings with parents and guardians several years ago, he's noticed a significant difference in his relationship with families. "Before, they used to question the value of Morning Meeting a lot. Now, more often than not, they want to tell me how much they appreciate what the students are learning in this daily routine—the social skills and the academic skills. Family involvement has also improved dramatically since I began using this structure for open houses. Now when I ask families for help with anything, they're there."

FROM THE SUMMER 2003 ISSUE OF THE *RESPONSIVE CLASSROOM* NEWSLETTER.

Taking the Rules
School-Wide

Traveling Rules

Helping children pay attention to classroom rules throughout the school: A question and answers from teachers

✦

QUESTION | *The classroom environment is calmer and friendlier when we work with the children to create classroom rules. But teachers still often get reports from lunch, recess, and special area teachers about problematic behaviors in those areas. How do you help children pay attention to your classroom rules even when they're not in the classroom?*

Tim Keefe has been teaching for eighteen years and is currently a third grade teacher at Washington School in West Haven, Connecticut.

ANSWER | I feel responsible for my class all day long, including during those times when I'm not with them, such as when they're riding the bus, lining up first thing in the morning, meeting with a special area teacher, or eating in the lunchroom. This means that our classroom rules are really rules for our life in school. I reinforce this idea in several ways.

For example, in the first weeks of school we'll talk in depth about how to pay attention to the classroom rules in the lunchroom. Sometimes I find it helpful to use a "T-chart" (see sample) that helps children think about what a particular rule might look like and sound like. What does it look like and sound like to be kind to your classmates at lunch? We use the T-chart to structure a discussion of the rule and then we model expected behaviors. We follow this with visits to the lunchroom, where we practice waiting in line, getting trays, sitting and talking, cleaning up our trays, etc. Throughout the year, we pause before going to the lunchroom and talk briefly about expectations for behavior.

Respect and take care of everyone, in the classroom and in other places in the building

L O O K S L I K E *(our actions)*	S O U N D S L I K E *(our words, voice, tone)*
✦ Let others join in (recess, class, cafeteria). ✦ Take turns. ✦ Walk quietly in the hallway. ✦ Listen when others speak. ✦ Raise your hand to speak after others are done speaking.	✦ Ask to play or participate. ✦ Ask for help. ✦ Ask questions that show we are listening. ✦ Use words that encourage. ✦ Speak kindly.

I also check in every day when the children return from lunch. I begin with questions such as "Tell me about lunch today. What happened?" I often get more stories about negative behavior than positive, such as "So and so punched me." I respond by asking how we can help support positive behavior. For example, I might say "How can we help each other keep our hands to ourselves?"

Finally, I invite lunch teachers to visit the classroom where we can discuss with them our rules and expectations. I also invite them to attend a Morning Meeting and share something about themselves, so students get to know them better.

Carolyn Bush has taught at K.T. Murphy Elementary School in Stamford, Connecticut, for six years. She taught fourth grade for many years and currently teaches fifth grade.

ANSWER | I find it's helpful to give children responsibility for living the rules throughout the school. One way I do this is by creating jobs specifically connected to reinforcing the rules. For example, one job is to be the rule bearer, whose task is to carry the rules from our classroom to our special area rooms, the lunchroom, and the playground (see the box, "Our Rules Go with Us Everywhere We Go").

Another job is line leader. The job rotates weekly, and two students always work together. Their job is to make sure that students line up and move through the halls quietly. In the classroom, the line leaders give a thumbs-up signal when the children are ready to leave the classroom. They then lead the line of children into the hallway. Outside the classroom, the line leaders pay attention to how the children are behaving. This means that the line leaders need to remember the rules.

Our Rules Go with Us
Everywhere We Go

FROM *RULES IN SCHOOL*, NORTHEAST FOUNDATION FOR CHILDREN, INC., 2003.

Tina Valentine, a fourth grade teacher at Kensington Elementary School in Springfield, Massachusetts, describes a way to literally carry the rules outside the classroom. In many classrooms at the school, one of the daily jobs is "rule bearer." This child is responsible for carrying a laminated poster of the classroom rules wherever the class goes. Whether the group goes to the auditorium for music, the gym for PE, or the library for research, the rule bearer brings the class-room rules along for posting. At the end of the period, the rule bearer carries the rules back to the classroom. "The traveling rules poster is a tangible reminder that no matter where students are or who is teaching them, their classroom rules still apply," says Valentine.

Fellow Kensington teacher Maureen Russell teaches first graders a ritual for handing off the rules poster, which she attaches to a coat hanger for easier carrying. Upon entering a special area, the rule bearer goes to the special area teacher and announces, "Here are our rules." The teacher responds, "I accept the rules of Room 10" and then hangs the rules in a prominent place.

But it takes more than simply carrying the rules from place to place to make this strategy effective. When introducing the idea of traveling rules to students, it's important to involve the special area teachers in the conversation from the start. And special area teachers need to rein-force the importance of living the rules. For example, the first time the traveling rules are received, the special area teacher might talk with students about what it looks like to follow these rules in the special area. The special area teacher might add one or two rules that are specific to that area. To achieve the greatest consistency, the special area teacher also uses the same signals for attention as the classroom teacher and follows the same procedures when a child doesn't follow the rules.

If anyone breaks the rules, the line leader asks them to step out of the line and walk behind me instead of behind the line leader. If it's one of the line leaders who forgets or chooses not to follow the rules, I intervene. That child cannot be line leader that day and the job shifts to the next child in line.

Before the line leaders can be successful, the class needs to discuss, model, and practice how to line up and how to move through the halls: line up quickly and quietly, stand without fidgeting, keep their eyes on the line leaders, step out of line and move behind me when the line leader asks them to, etc.

When I feel that the children are comfortable with lining up and walking in the halls, I then introduce the tasks of the line leader. Children discuss how to recognize that the line is ready to move out of the classroom. What does the line need to look like? Sound like? We model and practice the thumbs-up signal that indicates it's time to move into the hall. And we discuss, model, and practice what it looks and sounds like to respect the line leader.

Barbara Knoblock is a primary grades teacher at New Sarpy
Elementary School in Destrehan, Louisiana.

A N S W E R | I like to put rules in the larger context of the
positive social behavior that rules support—and it's this positive
behavior that I choose to focus on with the students. Sometime
during the first six weeks of school, I introduce character traits
such as responsibility, self-discipline, fairness, loyalty, and trust-
worthiness. I use literature and songs to introduce each trait
and to begin making the traits concrete and easy for the children
to understand. We then make word webs where we define the
character trait and describe what it looks like and sounds like
in action. We also role-play situations where we need to behave
fairly, responsibly, etc.; we act out skits with puppets; and we
make class books in which the students draw and write about
how they demonstrate the character traits at home and at school.

In all these activities, we're thinking about how we practice these
positive behaviors not only in the classroom but also in the
library, the cafeteria, and enrichment classes. For example, if I want
students to learn how to act responsibly in music class as well as
in our classroom, I might begin a discussion with them by asking,
"What are ways you can show responsibility in the music room?"
We then list, describe, and practice specific responsible behaviors
such as following directions and listening respectfully.

I have found that teaching character traits this way helps my
classes develop a better understanding of what these words
really mean. Then it's easier for them to carry this understanding into other areas of their lives.

FROM THE SPRING 2003 ISSUE OF THE *RESPONSIVE CLASSROOM* NEWSLETTER.

Buddy Teachers

Lending a hand to keep time-out positive and productive

BY ALICE YANG

NEFC EDITOR/WRITER

AND

RUTH SIDNEY CHARNEY

NEFC CO–FOUNDER AND *RESPONSIVE CLASSROOM*
CONSULTING TEACHER

I t's language arts time in Mr. Jeffrey's third grade class. The children have settled into their writing assignments. Mr. Jeffrey is working with a small group when he notices Lucia across the room distracting her neighbors with chatter.

"Lucia, do your work and let others do theirs," he says in an even voice. Lucia quiets down, but a moment later takes out some finger nail polish, starts doing her nails, and offers to do her neighbors'. "Lucia, time-out," Mr. Jeffrey says calmly and firmly. Lucia goes to the time-out area but protests angrily. While in time-out, she bangs her feet loudly against a nearby bookcase, mutters insults about the teacher, and tries to catch her classmates' eyes. After a minute or two of this, Mr. Jeffrey says to another student, "James, go tell Ms. Daniels that we need her." James quietly leaves the room, returning shortly with Ms. Daniels.

Upon Ms. Daniels's arrival, Mr. Jeffrey says to Lucia, "Go with Ms. Daniels now." Wordlessly, Ms. Daniels escorts Lucia to her own classroom for a time-out there while Mr. Jeffrey continues working with the class.

Mr. Jeffrey and Ms. Daniels are buddy teachers, a pair of teachers in nearby rooms who have agreed to lend each other a hand with time-out, a nonpunitive strategy for helping children regain their self-control. In most cases, time-out takes place in the children's own classroom: A child who is not following the rules is calmly and matter-of-factly reminded to go to a designated spot in the room for a minute or more to refocus before returning to the group. But for those times when a student refuses to go to time-out, continues to act out while there, or resumes disruptive behavior upon returning to the group, teachers need a simple and effective way to handle the situation. Buddy teacher time-out is one such method.

BENEFITS OF THE APPROACH

"Buddy teacher time-out can stop a negative cycle of behavior," says Gail Sperling, first and third grade teacher at Yavneh Day School in Cincinnati, Ohio. "Some children continue to be stimulated by the other students in the room when they're in time-out, even if the teacher has taught children to focus only on themselves during this time," she says. "A change of scenery can help those children settle down." Other children might continue to act out with regular time-out as a way of testing the system. In these cases, says Gail, buddy teacher time-out shows them that the expectations for behavior are firm.

Another important benefit of buddy teacher time-out is that it allows the teacher to continue working with the class. With the buddy teacher taking care of the child for the moment, the teacher can continue with the lesson as planned. This shows the child and the rest of the class that disruptive behavior isn't going to derail the class's work.

Finally, buddy teacher time-out can help the teacher stay calm as well. "When you're at the end of your rope," says Gail, "having a buddy take the child gives you some distance." Later, when the teacher and child are both calmer, they can talk more constructively about the incident.

TIPS FOR USING BUDDY TEACHER TIME-OUT

Teach the procedure ahead of time

As with regular time-out, it's important to teach children the buddy teacher time-out procedure explicitly and give them opportunities to practice it.

Susan Smith, a third grade teacher at Rolling Hills Elementary School in Holland, Pennsylvania, introduces the procedure during the first weeks of school after introducing regular time-out. Just as with regular time-out, she explains that the purpose of buddy teacher time-out is to help children regain self-control. Using a matter-of-fact tone of voice, she talks with the class about how sometimes a person goes to time-out and still can't get calm. "I tell the children, 'When time-out in our own room isn't enough, we can try going to another room.'"

Then the class practices. Susan invites any child who wants to try a pretend buddy teacher time-out to do so. This year, over the course of several weeks, more than half the class went one at a time to sit for a few minutes in the time-out area in the buddy teacher's room.

Susan and her buddy teacher also teach the rest of the class what to do if a classmate goes to a buddy teacher's room or a student comes to their room for a time-out. In both cases, the children are taught to keep doing what they were doing and not to interact with the child.

"All this practice makes the children feel that they know what to do, and it teaches them that time-out is for everyone," says Susan. It can help remove any stigma that children perceive around time-out, whether in their own room or another room.

Common Questions about Buddy Teacher Time-Out

Isn't this a hassle for the buddy teacher? Most teachers who have provided "buddy teacher service" say that the brief interruption is not a problem. Most children go to the buddy teacher's room quietly and recover quickly without incident. This is especially true if students in the buddy teacher's room know that their job is to leave the child alone.

Is it really safe for the buddy teacher to leave her/his class alone?
The two classrooms should be near each other so that the teacher only needs to be gone for about two minutes. The children should be taught that if their teacher needs to leave the room, then it's serious and their job is to keep working. If a teacher feels, however, that it's not safe to leave the room, another adult, such as someone from the office, should take the child to the buddy teacher's room.

Wouldn't it be simpler to have the child go to the buddy teacher's room alone? For safety's sake, it's important to keep an upset child within adult sight. Left alone, an upset child may never make it to the buddy teacher's room, may deface the hallway or bathroom, or may go outside the building.

What if the teacher her/himself escorts the child to the buddy teacher's room? The trouble is that this pulls the teacher's attention away from the class. It could also send the message that disruptive behavior gets more attention from the teacher than cooperative behavior.

Isn't it embarrassing for a student to have to leave one classroom and walk into another one? Children often feel bad when they're not functioning well in a group. Teachers can't and shouldn't try to take away all the uncomfortable feelings. But they can prevent a child from feeling further humiliated by the time-out procedure if they explicitly teach it to the class, have all the children practice it, and maintain a matter-of-fact demeanor when using it. Something else that helps is reminding children often that we all forget the rules sometimes and that time-out is a way to help us get back on track while keeping the group safe.

Keep the talk to a minimum

In the opening example, Mr. Jeffrey does not argue, cajole, coax, or reason with Lucia. He simply gives her clear, brief instructions. The less the teacher engages with the student in this situation, the less interruption to the work of the class.

Similarly, Mr. Jeffrey does not make any extraneous comments to the messenger student or to Ms. Daniels. And Ms. Daniels does not ask what happened. She does not express sympathy for Lucia or scold her in any way. The job of the buddy teacher is to provide a safe haven for the student, not to interact with the child or process the incident. In any case, attempts to process or draw conclusions are seldom productive at this point.

Even the students are taught to be brief and to the point when they're asked to go get the buddy teacher. "Mr. Jeffrey needs you" or "Mr. Jeffrey says to please come to our room," a child might say, and leave it at that.

Show welcome when the child returns

After a while, perhaps at the end of the class period, the classroom teacher goes to the buddy teacher's room. If the child has regained control and is ready to rejoin the class, the two return to the classroom together. It's important at this point to convey welcome to the child and show that s/he is still liked and valued. "Have a seat at your desk, Lucia. We've just started our fish observations. I'll be over to help you in a minute," Mr. Jeffrey says with a smile. This conveys warmth and communicates Mr. Jeffrey's belief that Lucia can and will get back on task. Later, when Lucia and Mr. Jeffrey are both prepared to talk, they discuss what led to the need for a time-out. Mr. Jeffrey realizes that Lucia is a struggling writer and needs more support to initiate writing. The two talk about how Lucia will get that support in the future.

A REALITY OF TEACHING

Teachers sometimes worry that needing to rely on a buddy teacher for help is a sign of incompetence. On the contrary, it's a sign of recognizing the reality of teaching. It's a simple fact that some children and some situations require greater intervention than can be provided by a single teacher who also needs to continue teaching the rest of the class. Turning to a colleague for help is a perfectly responsible way to make sure all children get the care and attention they need.

FROM THE WINTER 2005 ISSUE OF THE *RESPONSIVE CLASSROOM* NEWSLETTER.

A Place for Recovering Self-Control

BY CHIP WOOD

NEFC CO-FOUNDER AND PRINCIPAL AT SHEFFIELD ELEMENTARY SCHOOL

TURNERS FALLS, MASSACHUSETTS

"One more peep out of you and you're going to the principal's office!"

Who among us didn't hear these words from our teachers when we were growing up? Who among us hasn't been tempted, when our patience has worn thin, to use them ourselves in our teaching?

Traditionally, the first thing teachers do when a student acts out is to send the student to the office. They may very well do this with good intentions. The child needs to regain self-control, the thinking may go, and removing the child from the scene of agitation

93

can help the child do that. Or sending students to the office may be the teachers' way of keeping themselves from doing or saying something to escalate the tension. Better to hand the situation over to someone who isn't, at the moment, fed up.

All too often, however, teachers send students to the office out of anger. The method then becomes a way to trump the student, an "I'll show you!" form of authority.

Whatever the intention, the trouble with sending students to the office is that it often doesn't solve any problems.

Typically, students sent to the office are told to sit on a bench in the reception area, a bench with a long history. Students, parents, secretaries, custodians, even the postal workers who come and go know what it means if you're sitting on the bench. It means you're *In Trouble*. And you, enduring the looks of every passerby, sit there and worry because you're about to go in and be punished by the principal.

So, where could students go, if not the principal's office, when a change of setting is needed?

A DESIGNATED PLACE FOR REGAINING SELF-CONTROL

Some schools have a buddy teacher system, whereby each teacher partners with another who can help out when a child is losing self-control. When a child has had a time-out in his/her own classroom but continues to have trouble, the child goes for a time-out in the buddy teacher's classroom. Often this change of setting enables the child to regain composure. But what if it doesn't? What's the next step?

In some schools, the answer is a special room purposely infused with an atmosphere of regrouping, problem solving, and learning. Called various names, such as the Student Resource Center, Back-on-Track Room, and Rest and Recovery Room, the place is staffed by a teacher, interventionist, counselor, specialist, or other adult member of the school. When a time-out in the classroom doesn't help a student, the student goes to a buddy teacher's room. And when time-out in the buddy teacher's room doesn't help, the student goes to this special room.

The purpose of sending students to this room is not to punish them. The role of the adult staffing this room is to help the student cool down and, a little later, reflect on or talk about the incident that just happened. The adult also helps the student plan and perhaps rehearse what to do or say when the classroom teacher is ready for the student to come back to the classroom.

ONE SCHOOL'S APPROACH

In one semi-rural school in New England, the idea of a safe, separate place to help students regain self-control energized both the principal and the staff. Working together, they named an underused classroom the Student Resource Center and found ways to make sure that the room would never be without an adult who could receive a student.

In one half of the Student Resource Center, the staff installed four office cubicles for use by Title I teachers, a guidance counselor, classroom teachers, and the principal. Equipped with doors, walls that were glass from waist height up, phones, and computers, the cubicles were quiet places for planning, teaching, and both academic and social learning.

Worktables, reading chairs, two student computer stations, and some library materials occupied the other half of the room. This was the area to which the supervising adult would direct a child who needed to recover composure. "Come over here and have a seat," the adult would say, and then leave the child alone. The goal at this point was to give the child space to calm down, not to engage in conversation.

Later, when the student had regained composure, the adult would come over for a talk. "It looks like you've calmed down. Would you like to talk about what happened?" The adult's job was to listen and provide prompts. "What are some things you could do differently if this happens again?" the adult would ask. "What's something you might want to say to your teacher when she talks to you about this? What's something that would be helpful to hear from your teacher? How might she help you with this back in your classroom?" Only after a conversation like this would the student return to the classroom.

TWO KEYS TO SUCCESS

The Student Resource Center at this school was part of a larger effort among the staff to address discipline in a proactive and nonpunitive way. It owed much of its success to this larger effort. But two specific things about the Student Resource Center itself are worth noting.

First, the adults staffing the room at any given time, whoever they were, saw themselves as part of a school-wide team, not just as individual staff members with separate responsibilities. Not enough can be said about this spirit of cooperation, mutual respect, and trust among the adults at school. In safe, challenging, and joyful schools, trust among staff is evident in routine interactions as well as in tough situations of stress or conflict. Through these trusting relationships, teachers are able to proactively make changes to improve school climate and children's academic and social learning.

The second noteworthy thing about this school's Student Resource Center is that the students and staff generally understood the positive purpose of the space. Overall, the room was perceived as a place for students to get a little extra help on a research project or a book report. Students could also ask to go to the Student Resource Center if they needed a quiet space to work or a place to go at the beginning of the day. Yes, this was where you came if you lost your self-control, but kids would be here for lots of different reasons, and all of you were here to learn something, be it something social or academic or both. Unlike the traditional principal's office, the Student Resource Center was about getting help and about learning.

OTHER POSSIBLE SPACES

Certainly, not many schools have an underused classroom, or even an underused closet. What other spaces might a school use as a student recovery area? Here are some possibilities:

✦ **The computer lab** The computer screen often provides refuge for mildly upset children. It might be effective to set aside one or two stations in the computer lab for children who need to regain self-control, if the lab can be staffed by more than one teacher or a teacher and assistant. One of the adults would then guide the student in recovering self-control and preparing to re-enter the classroom.

✦ **The library or media center** Could you use some portion of the space as a recovery area? The library or media center, with its emphasis on learning and its typically quiet and tranquil atmosphere, may be a good setting for children needing redirection.

✦ **A conference room** Do you have a conference room next to the principal's office or elsewhere that's sparingly used? Could you arrange for it to double as a student recovery space?

THE WORRY OF "REWARDING" STUDENTS

Sometimes people worry that time spent in a Student Resource Center or the computer lab will feel like a reward to a student. What about the child who "just wants to get out of doing his work," or the one who prefers the resource room because "all they do there is play"? Aren't we just rewarding these students for bad behavior? Won't they continue to act out so they can go to these places more often?

No, they will not—provided that we keep working hard to make our classrooms safe, joyful places in which children feel respected and supported. These are the kinds of classrooms to which students want to return. The truth is that children who are getting what they need in a classroom do not want to leave it for very long, no matter how attractive the recovery area.

Whatever our role in the school—teacher, counselor, principal, school nurse, librarian, recovery room staff—we all share the same goal: for the child to regain self-control and re-enter the classroom as quickly and effectively as possible. To make that happen, we need to understand why children behave the way they do. Saying that a child "just wants to get out of doing his work" may be an accurate description of the child's behavior, but we still haven't solved the child's problem. To do that, we need to ask ourselves *why* questions:

✦ Why does Scott want to avoid his work? Is it too hard for him? Too easy? Too confusing? Are his peers teasing him because he's having trouble understanding?

✦ Why does Molly prefer "playing" in the resource room to working in her own classroom? Does she need help relating to other children? Is she getting enough sleep? What kind of classroom work seems to engage her? Does she need more direct reassurance and support?

Why questions lead naturally to *what* and *how* questions:

✦ What might we be doing to trigger the cycle of events that leads the child to the recovery room—a cycle that some children seem to get caught in again and again?

✦ How can we change our own behavior to avoid power struggles with the child?

✦ How can we respond differently when the child pushes our buttons?

✦ What do we need to change to help this child stay engaged and working productively in the classroom?

✦ How can we help children have incremental successes—to do just a bit better each day in learning how to manage their work, their feelings, and their responses to the school environment?

Finding answers to these questions is simple for some children and much more difficult for others. The important thing is to keep asking. The recovery area is there as a backup as you work your way toward answers, and using it does not represent failure for either teacher or child. Instead, it signals to students, teachers, and families that the school has many positive ways to help all children get what they need so that they can learn.

SETTING THE STAGE FOR GROWTH

Working creatively as a team, every school can move away from the office bench toward a space in the school where respect and recovery set the stage for improved student behavior and increased academic engagement. Where there is a collective will, there can be a community way.

School-Wide Rules Creation

A landmark in a 14-month journey to improve school climate

BY KEVIN WHITE

SCHOOL COUNSELOR AT SHEFFIELD ELEMENTARY SCHOOL
TURNERS FALLS, MASSACHUSETTS

AND

CHIP WOOD

NEFC CO–FOUNDER AND PRINCIPAL AT SHEFFIELD ELEMENTARY SCHOOL
TURNERS FALLS, MASSACHUSETTS

Sheffield Elementary, a grade 3–6 school in Turners Falls, Massachusetts, faced a challenge familiar to many educators: how to develop a more consistent approach to discipline from classroom to classroom and in common school areas, such as the playground, lunchroom, and hallways.

In the fall of 2003, our school community had identified ensuring a positive school climate as a top priority. We wanted to devise consistent, school-wide disciplinary policies to help children follow school-wide rules. These policies would apply to all behavior, whether occurring within or beyond the classroom. Next, we needed to help the children create the school-wide rules. Then we had to help them learn what following those rules would look like, feel like, and sound like. What, for example, does a common rule such as "Be kind" look, feel, and sound like for children sharing the lunchroom space?

All of these steps were integral to improving the school climate. The step that this article will focus on is the creation of the school-wide rules, undertaken with students in fall 2004, the second year of our project. Students, parents, teachers, counselor, and principal worked hard together to create a Sheffield "Constitution"—a set of school-wide behavioral guidelines distilled from separate sets of classroom rules. As our second year progressed, we began to see some positive results: Our use of common teacher and student language about behavior and rules, the emphasis on teacher modeling, and a great deal of practice in living our constitution all helped make the school climate more peaceful and productive.

Schools will find many ways to do the hard work of developing school-wide rules, depending on the ages and needs of their students. Here is what the process looked like at Sheffield.

ARE WE READY?

We adults (principal, counselor, teachers, support staff, and parents) began our work formally in January 2004, well before we involved the students. We asked ourselves two key questions about our readiness to help the children formulate and follow school-wide rules:

1 Did we have a clear set of disciplinary policies that let everyone know how to help children who had trouble following the rules?

2 Did the children know how to formulate and follow rules in their own classrooms?

Disciplinary policies: In place before school started

In January 2004, a task force made up of teachers, other staff, and parents began exploring what a school-wide discipline plan would look like. The task force set up discussions with the entire staff and surveyed parents, staff, and the whole student body (over 270 students). They received written responses from 243 students, 104 parents, and 43 out of 55 staff. The active involvement of so many members of the school community was important, given the size and complexity of the project.

One outcome of the discussions was the creation of a set of disciplinary guidelines for handling children's behavior problems anywhere in the school. The guidelines were eventually included in the parent-student handbook, which we sent home with students in September of the 2004/05 school year. These guidelines included "Steps to Self-Control" that would help children get back on track when they were having trouble following classroom or school-wide rules (see box on page 104).

Classroom rules: Created

At the start of the 2004/05 school year, each class had created their own classroom rules (see box on page 107). By late September, the classes had been learning and living with those rules for several weeks.

Steps to Self-Control

from the Sheffield Elementary School Parent-Student Handbook

The following steps usually help children manage their behavior in both classroom and nonclassroom areas. When these steps are not enough, the handbook goes on to discuss keeping students after school for social skills tutoring with the principal or extra homework help. Suspension (either in or out of school, depending upon child and family needs), is still used for serious misconduct.

1 When children begin to lose control, teachers remind them of the rules and, if necessary, calmly and concisely redirect their actions. For example, to a child disrupting another student's work, a teacher might say, "Take your work to that table, please."

2 If children continually choose to ignore or are so upset that they cannot follow the rules, they need a few minutes in a safe place to cool down. This "Take A Break" area may be within the children's classroom. Sometimes taking a break in a buddy teacher's classroom is used as a next step.

3 If children continue acting out, they need to spend more time in a quiet place. In our Peace Room, upset students can focus on structured problem-solving without distractions, do assigned classroom work, and interrupt a pattern of nonproductive behavior. They stay in the Peace Room until they show their readiness to be welcomed back into the classroom

Teachers and staff adapt these steps for use in the lunchroom, hallways, and other school spaces. For example, a child who is becoming too noisy at lunch may be told to go for a calming-down break in the Peace Room, which is right across the hall.

Any nearby adult member of the school community will take responsibility for guiding children through these steps to self-control.

CREATING OUR CONSTITUTION

At the end of September 2004, after fourteen months of working hard together, we had classroom rules and a set of clear disciplinary policies in place. Finally, we were ready for the children to consider what safe, respectful behavior would look like inside and outside the classroom. It was time to create the Sheffield Constitution.

To enhance academic learning as the children worked on their school-wide rules, we decided to guide them through the same sort of democratic process that resulted in the creation of the U.S. Constitution in 1787. In the classrooms, teachers noted that our school's rule-making process was similar to the one by which our nation's founders had created the most important laws of our country. Social skills were bolstered as children from all classes and grades worked together.

The grade-level mini-convention

Each of the school's fourteen classes chose two delegates to represent them at a grade-level mini-convention. The job of the delegates at each grade-level mini-convention was to discuss all the classroom rules for their grade and select three to five upon which all could agree. We felt that as an important part of the students' learning, they should have some say in how they would arrive at their grade-level rules, as long as their method was fair and respectful. Some delegates voted rule by rule for inclusion or exclusion. Others grouped similar rules so that they could more easily decide among them. One grade felt it important to include at least one rule from each classroom.

The mini-convention delegates talked about what the words they were using meant—words such as "respect" and "responsibility."

One group of students said that respect meant "listen when the teacher's talking; don't talk back." Another group said that respect meant "be nice to everybody."

Students also discussed what it would look, sound, and feel like to follow the rules they were crafting. "If Rebecca were being kind to Simon during math," the adults asked, "what might she say if he made a mistake?" One student said, "She could say, 'How did you get that answer, Simon?'" Another student suggested that Rebecca could say, "I have another idea, Simon. Would you like to hear it?"

By the end of the mini-convention, we had four sets of three to five rules, one set for each of the grades in our school. We were ready for the next step.

On to the Constitutional Convention

Before adjourning, the classroom delegates decided which two delegates would represent their whole grade at the Sheffield Constitutional Convention. On September 27, 2004, these eight grade-level delegates, along with the school counselor and principal, set off for "Philadelphia"—the superintendent's conference room on the other side of our complex. After a formal greeting and words of encouragement from superintendent Sue Gee, the delegates got down to the business of transforming four sets of grade-level rules (a total of approximately sixteen rules) into one set of three to five school-wide rules.

Taking their responsibility quite seriously, the delegates reviewed and discussed and struggled to find a way to reduce the many rules down to just three to five. They tried choosing rules from the various class posters. They tried categorizing and grouping rules that were similar. We (their principal and counselor, the only

From Hopes and Dreams to Classroom Rules

In classrooms using the *Responsive Classroom* approach, teachers work with the children to create the classroom rules. Generated from students' ideas, these rules set limits and boundaries in a way that fosters group ownership and self-discipline.

Rule creation takes place in the early weeks of school. Here is what the process typically looks like.

1 Articulating hopes and dreams The teacher helps students set goals for the year, often beginning by sharing her/his own goals for the year.

2 Generating rules Teacher and students collaborate to generate rules that allow all class members to achieve their hopes and dreams.

3 Framing the rules in the positive The teacher works with students to turn rules about what *not* to do into rules about what *to* do; for example, "Don't run" might become "Move safely."

4 Condensing the list The teacher helps students consolidate their long list of specific rules into three to five broad classroom rules. Students make a poster of the rules and display it prominently in the room.

Teachers find over and over that this investment of time and effort is well worth the payoff: calm, productive, and joyful classrooms.

adults present) offered suggestions and gentle guidance. But the first hour passed and the delegates had not agreed on a single rule.

At this point, we offered the delegates a challenge: We would leave the room and return in five to ten minutes. The delegates' task: Agree on the most important rule and write it on the chart paper. We checked in at the end of five minutes and were told "Not yet!" We were worried: Would this work? Was the task too big? Would the children be able to come up with even that first rule? After another ten nerve-wracking minutes, we were welcomed back into the room. There on the paper was one word in big, bold letters: ENJOY!

The delegates were excited. We adults were pleasantly surprised by the concise and powerful first rule. But we were still worried: Would the children finish the rest of the rule-making successfully? We were politely told to "go away again." The students would work on the second rule and tell us when they were ready. We waited in the hall. Each time we checked, we were told "Not yet!" As school dismissal time approached, we began to wonder if the task could be completed on time.

Finally, we were signaled back in. Expecting to see only rule two added below rule one, we were delighted to see instead five rules and a very satisfied-looking group of delegates. After about an hour and a half of serious deliberation, fourteen sets of rules crafted by over 270 students were now represented by one set

Student delegates at Sheffield Elementary School created school-wide rules to help everyone in the school maintain safe and caring behavior. Here they stand with principal Chip Wood at the all-school celebration.

of proposed school-wide rules: Following "Enjoy!" we saw "Respect everyone and everything around you, Speak kindly, Be helpful and responsible, Take care of classrooms and school property." The delegates were now ready to present their work to the school community.

The rules ratification ceremony

On October 6, 2004, the whole student body assembled in the auditorium along with teachers, parents, principal, counselor, and official guests. All the rules from which the school-wide rules had been distilled—the fourteen classroom rules posters and the four sets of grade-level rules—were displayed at the front of the auditorium.

Mr. White, the school counselor, asked all the students, teachers, and other school staff to stand. "Everyone you see standing here," he said, "participated in creating the classroom rules that are the foundation for the school-wide rules we will ratify today." The whole auditorium rang with enthusiastic applause. Mr. White then heightened the excitement by asking everyone to be seated except for the two delegates from each of the fourteen classrooms. After another big round of applause, Mr. White asked these twenty-eight students to be seated and turned everyone's attention to the stage, where the eight grade-level delegates sat with the superintendent of schools, school committee chair, fire and police chiefs, town select board, and other local officials. Behind them hung a giant poster of the Sheffield Rules, which had been commercially produced to emphasize the importance of the occasion.

Mr. White described the long and careful process these eight delegates had followed to distill the school-wide rules from so many sets of classroom rules. Then he invited the delegates to explain each school-wide rule. "Rule one," they said. "Enjoy. That means enjoy learning, enjoy your classmates, enjoy your teachers, enjoy recess, enjoy school." In similar fashion, they explained each of the remaining four rules. When they finished, the rules were affirmed by voice vote and a stirring standing ovation. Invited guests congratulated the delegates on their accomplishment. The guests also reminded all of the students that for the work they had done to be meaningful, the whole school community (children and adults) would need to help one another learn and live by the constitution in the months ahead.

Posting and distributing copies of the constitution

After the ratification ceremony, smaller versions of the Sheffield Rules poster were given to staff for posting in classrooms and in the hallways, lunchroom, library, and other common school areas. In the classrooms, teachers helped children see how the Sheffield Rules were similar to their own classrooms rules. For example, a teacher might say, "The Sheffield Rules are the ones we follow when we're outside our classroom. They have the same ideas as our classroom rules, although some of the words are different." The teacher might then guide the children through a comparison of words and ideas to help them relate the two sets of rules. Parents also received copies of the school-wide rules with reminders of which pages in the parent-student handbook would apply when any of these rules was broken.

Moving into the future

We know our school-wide rules need to belong not just to the students present in our constitutional year, but to all the students following them. That means discussion, modeling, and practice of the rules as we welcome new children each year. It also means ongoing communication among all the adults of the school community. Sharing insights and observations is the best way to know if the rules are helping us meet our hopes and dreams for all the children.

WHAT WE ACCOMPLISHED

Creating school-wide rules and disciplinary policies helped Sheffield Elementary School take a huge step toward resolving concerns about school climate. Engaging all of the children in the rule-setting process helped them take ownership of the rules. Engaging all of the adults emphasized for the children the significance of their work. Together, we are creating a calmer, happier place for learning.

FROM THE NOVEMBER 2005 ISSUE OF THE *RESPONSIVE CLASSROOM* NEWSLETTER.

In the resources listed here, you'll find more detailed information on ideas and practices discussed in this book as well as general information about the *Responsive Classroom®* approach to teaching. To access any article or order any book, video, or pamphlet, go to the *Responsive Classroom* website, www.responsiveclassroom.org.

UNDERSTANDING CHILDREN'S DEVELOPMENT

Bechtel, Lynn. "How Old Are You? Knowing children's developmental stages helps teachers plan for the year." In the Summer 2002 issue of the *Responsive Classroom* newsletter.

Greene, Ross W. 2001. *The Explosive Child: A New Approach for Understanding and Parenting Easily Frustrated, Chronically Inflexible Children.* New York: HarperCollins.

NEFC staff members. 1993. *A Notebook for Teachers: Making Changes in the Elementary Curriculum* (based on developmentally appropriate practice). Greenfield, Massachusetts: Northeast Foundation for Children, Inc.

Wood, Chip. 1997. *Yardsticks: Children in the Classroom Ages 4–14.* Greenfield, Massachusetts: Northeast Foundation for Children, Inc.

THE FIRST SIX WEEKS OF SCHOOL

"Building a Sense of Ownership: Teachers share ideas for the early weeks of school." In the Spring 2000 issue of the *Responsive Classroom* newsletter.

Denton, Paula, and Roxann Kriete. 2000. *The First Six Weeks of School.* Greenfield, Massachusetts: Northeast Foundation for Children, Inc.

Olivera, Elisabeth. "Getting to Know You: Ideas for helping children feel comfortable in their first weeks of school." In the Summer 1998 issue of the *Responsive Classroom* newsletter.

MORNING MEETING

"Activity Ideas for News and Announcements Charts." In the Spring 2005 issue of the *Responsive Classroom* newsletter.

Bondy, Elizabeth, and Sharon Ketts. "The Power of Morning Meeting: 'Like Being at the Breakfast Table.'" In the Fall 2001 issue of the *Responsive Classroom* newsletter.

Correa-Connolly, Melissa. 2004. *99 Activities and Greetings.* Turners Falls, Massachusetts: Northeast Foundation for Children, Inc.

Doing Morning Meeting (30 min., VHS color video). 2004. Greenfield, Massachusetts and Portland, Maine: Northeast Foundation for Children, Inc., and Stenhouse Publishers.

Kriete, Roxann, with contributions by Lynn Bechtel. 2002. *The Morning Meeting Book.* 2nd ed. Greenfield, Massachusetts: Northeast Foundation for Children, Inc.

Kriete, Roxann. "Morning Meeting: A Powerful Way to Begin the Day." In the Winter 1999 issue of the *Responsive Classroom* newsletter.

"Themed Sharing during Morning Meeting." In the August 2005 issue of the *Responsive Classroom* newsletter.

RULES AND LOGICAL CONSEQUENCES

Brady, Kathryn, Mary Beth Forton, Deborah Porter, and Chip Wood. 2003. *Rules in School.* Greenfield, Massachusetts: Northeast Foundation for Children, Inc.

Brady, Kathryn, Mary Beth Forton, Deborah Porter, and Chip Wood. "Bringing Classroom Rules to Life." In the Spring 2003 issue of the *Responsive Classroom* newsletter.

Nelsen, Jane. *Positive Discipline.* 1996. New York: Random House.

GUIDED DISCOVERY

Bechtel, Lynn, and Paula Denton. "Guided Discovery in Action." In the Summer 2004 issue of the *Responsive Classroom* newsletter.

Denton, Paula. 2005. *Learning Through Academic Choice.* Turners Falls, Massachusetts: Northeast Foundation for Children, Inc.

Denton, Paula. "Academic Choice: A powerful tool for motivating and maximizing students' learning." In the Spring 2005 issue of the *Responsive Classroom* newsletter.

"Favorite Guided Discoveries." In the Summer 2004 issue of the *Responsive Classroom* newsletter.

ACADEMIC CHOICE

Denton, Paula. "Academic Choice: A powerful tool for motivating and maximizing students' learning." In the Spring 2005 issue of the *Responsive Classroom* newsletter.

Denton, Paula. 2005. *Learning Through Academic Choice.* Turners Falls, Massachusetts: Northeast Foundation for Children, Inc.

Fisher, Rosalea. "Choosing Choice." In the Fall 2001 issue of the *Responsive Classroom* newsletter.

WORKING WITH PARENTS

Davis, Carol, and Alice Yang. 2005. *Parents & Teachers Working Together.* Turners Falls, Massachusetts: Northeast Foundation for Children, Inc.

Muller, Kathrine. "Keeping Connected: Ideas for maintaining a strong home-and-school connection throughout the school year." In the Winter 2004 issue of the *Responsive Classroom* newsletter.

Porter, Deborah. "Bridging Home and School." In the Summer 2004 issue of the *Responsive Classroom* newsletter.

Wood, Chip. "Families' Hopes and Dreams." September 1, 2003. *Responsive Classroom* website article library.

CLASSROOM SETUP

Clayton, Marlynn K., with Mary Beth Forton. 2001. *Classroom Spaces That Work.* Greenfield, Massachusetts: Northeast Foundation for Children, Inc.

Lord, Jay. "Lessons from the Apartment Classroom." June 1, 2002. *Responsive Classroom* website article library. (Adapted from *Classrooms Spaces That Work*, by Marlynn K. Clayton with Mary Beth Forton, Northeast Foundation for Children, Inc., Greenfield, Massachusetts, 2001.)

Porter, Deborah. "A Quiet Place for Rough Moments." In the Spring 2003 issue of the *Responsive Classroom* newsletter.

Robert, Gayle. "The Difference is Amazing: After 17 years in the classroom, a first grade teacher makes 'drastic' changes in the physical arrangement of the classroom." In the Spring 2001 issue of the *Responsive Classroom* newsletter.

Northeast Foundation for Children, Inc. (NEFC) is a
nonprofit educational organization whose mission is to
foster safe, challenging, and joyful elementary classrooms and
schools. NEFC develops and promotes the *Responsive Classroom*
approach to teaching, which offers educators practical
strategies for bringing together social and academic
learning throughout the school day.

NEFC offers workshops for teachers,
a newsletter and website, books and other resources,
and on-site services for schools and school districts.
For more information, please contact:

Responsive Classroom®

Northeast Foundation for Children, Inc.
85 Avenue A, Suite 204
P. O. Box 718
Turners Falls, MA 01376-0718

800-360-6332
www.responsiveclassroom.org

✦